Kharkiv

Written by Olena Zvychaina
Translated from Ukrainian
by J Zurowsky
Edited by Danny Evanishen
Illustrations and Design by Dorene Fehr

Published by
Ethnic Enterprises
Publishing Division
Summerland, BC

Canadian Cataloguing in Publication Data

Zvychaina, Olena.
 Kharkiv

Translation of: Zolotyi potichok z holodnoho Kharkova.
ISBN 0-9697448-6-9

I. Evanishen, Danny, 1945- II. Title.
PG3979.Z8Z313 1996   C891.7'933   C96-910096-5

Ethnic Enterprises
Publishing Division
Box 234
Summerland, BC
V0H 1Z0

Printed and Bound in Canada
by New Horizon Printers
Summerland, BC

1 2 3 4 5 6 7 8 9 10 • 05 04 03 02 01 2000 99 98 97 96

The Writer

Olena Zvychaina was born in Ukraine near the beginning of the 1900's. A reclusive individual whose exact birthdate is unknown, she died on Staten Island, New York in 1985. In the late 1920's, the first mention of her as a writer is found in various Soviet Ukrainian journals. However, only when she came to North America did she begin to make a major impression on the Ukrainian literary scene.

The Golden Stream Out of Hungry Kharkiv, from which this book was translated, was her first work in the West. Originally published in Winnipeg, Manitoba in 1947, it is the first of her many works dealing with wartime and interwar life in the former Soviet Union. Other works by her include *Myrhorod Fair* (1953), *Fear* (1957-8) and *You* (1982).

The Translator

J Zurowsky has studied Ukrainian literature concentrating on the Twentieth Century Ukrainian avant garde movement. He has had other translations and original works published in *The Well* and elsewhere.

The Editor/Publisher

Danny Evanishen has been writing and publishing books for a number of years. His other works include collections of Ukrainian folk tales retold in English and a collection of humorous short stories about Ukrainian pioneers in Canada.

The Illustrator

Dorene Fehr has been interested in art in its various forms since she was a child. Her previously published work can be seen in *Vuiko Yurko The First Generation.*

Permission for this translation was granted by the Shevchenko Scientific Society, Inc of New York, New York, who are the executors of Olena Zvychaina's estate.

Notes from the Translator

In 1939, before the outbreak of World War II, Kharkiv had a population of 833,000. It had witnessed years of Stalinist terror during which people were arrested, deported or executed for holding beliefs contrary to those of the Stalinist establishment. Among those to perish were the intellectual and artistic élite, people known personally by Olena Zvychaina. These years of terror during the interwar period became the subject of most of Olena Zvychaina's work in the West. The one exception is *The Golden Stream Out of Hungry Kharkiv*, which takes place during the war.

This story, it seems, happened either to somebody very close to Zvychaina, or perhaps to Zvychaina herself. Nevertheless, the traumas and tragedies of the Stalinist years, compounded by the atrocities of World War II, had a searing effect on Zvychaina. She became a recluse.

Kharkiv was occupied by the Germans on October 25, 1941, and they held the city for twenty-two months. The city they conquered was in ruins. The retreating Red Army had destroyed all the power stations, water supply systems, railways and other transportation and communication facilities. 400,000 people were evacuated from Kharkiv to Southern Asia for the duration of the war. The thousands who were held in NKVD prisons for political, social, religious and other beliefs were executed.

During the first three months of 1942, the period during which the bulk of the story takes place, it is estimated that 14,000 people died of starvation. The Nazis also started their own terror campaign, executing real and supposed Ukrainian nationalists, along with supporters of the previous régime and Jews. By the time the Soviet army retook Kharkiv, a further 100,000 people had been exterminated by the Nazis and their supporters. The Germans also transported 60,000 people to work in the forced labor camps in Germany.

The Red Army, then, entered a city with a remaining population of only 160-190,000 people. Soviet special police forces, upon the recapture of the city, proceeded to pursue suspected collaborators and Ukrainian nationalists, imprisoning and executing them.

Olena Zvychaina was one of the many Ukrainians transported to work in the German labor camps, and she ended up as one of the multitudinous Displaced Persons after World War II ended. She was able to emigrate to North America, where she and her husband led a very reclusive lifestyle, shunning contact with most of the Ukrainian community.

—J Zurowsky, 1996

The wind twirls the snow, wildly carrying snowflakes on his light wings; he plays.... Playing, he instills his own order on the streets.... Here on the corner of Pushkin and Kapluniv Streets, he constructs a complete snow fortress, while on the other side of Pushkin, he conscientiously sweeps the snow, as if with a broom, exposing a slippery and bare, ice-covered spot.... And Frost, the Joker himself, is playing; he pinches the air with, for Kharkiv, an unprecedented low temperature of minus 38 degrees Centigrade....

Down the center of Pushkin Street two women lumber a small sleigh toward Pushkin Cemetery, one harnessed to the sleigh in front, the other pushing from behind.... On the sleigh, tightly fastened with a thick rope, lies a corpse wrapped in a gray blanket.... Its legs hang from the sleigh rigid and unbendable, like two logs.... Two weird, thick stumps protrude from beneath the gray blanket....

This funeral does not arouse any curiosity from the many pedestrians.... Preoccupied, they run quickly past, huddled, hiding as deeply as possible their blue, generally puffy faces beneath the collars of their coats....

On the windswept and ice-covered spots, the sleigh with the corpse slides by itself and the two women run after it, fruitlessly trying to catch up to the corpse, which bravely glides toward the cemetery, having stuck out its weird thick stumps of numb legs....

Professor Vsevolod, tall and lanky with a pale nervous face, was dressed in a warm coat and fur hat; he seemed welded with his observant gaze to the corpse's weird, thick stumps. With his inherent absentmindedness, he did not listen to what his companion said. She was a short young woman with dark brows and a pleasant but pale and tired face; she spoke, but he did not hear. Professor Vsevolod was lost in his own thoughts.

After gliding over the ice-covered spot, the corpse in the sleigh stopped, politely waited for the two women, and in a moment travelled further with their help.

The professor, not breaking his diligent gaze from the body's thick stumps, deliberately took the young woman's arm to help her cross the bare-as-a-forehead slippery spot.

"You simply cannot imagine, Katrusia, how interesting the problem of hunger is from a scientific perspective," he said, evidently answering his own thoughts, which were completely different from what Katrusia spoke of. She took a quick, wondering glance at the scholar, not understanding what had changed the theme and direction of their debate.

"Precisely now, the winter of 1941-42, has become the time for a definitive study of the problem of hunger. A terrible time and full of tragedy! But the death of a large mass of humanity from hunger provides doctors with rich material for valuable scientific observation. I carefully follow my starving patients and I observe the changes which occur in their organisms, from the physical, as well as the physiological side.

"But for me the most interesting changes are those which take place in the person's psychological state. Precisely this is the theme of my latest research work, which I am now writing; specifically, the radical changes in a person's psychological state, which take place in the period of bloating from hunger."

Having hidden her nose in her fur collar, Katrusia intently listened to assistant Professor Vsevolod and gazed straight ahead. In the background covered by the trampled snow of Pushkin Street, she saw the sleigh with the body, and two female figures.

The corpse lazily neared the cemetery and the weird, thick stumps of its legs continuously miraged before Katrusia's eyes. She listened intently to Assistant Professor Vsevolod, now understanding, precisely, that these deceased legs, bloated from hunger, reminded the academic of a whole series of thoughts on a topic of interest to him.

Katrusia did not pay any specific attention to this corpse. So many of them were driven down Pushkin Street in the direction of the cemetery! Almost all were driven on sleighs, without a casket, plainly tied in some kind of rags. Sometimes they shipped the body only in underwear, covered with a sack, or a sheet. One can become accustomed to almost anything! Katrusia, living on Lermontov Street, not far from Pushkin Cemetery, was used to the sight — a sleigh directed toward the cemetery with the deceased, without a casket, in the company of one or two of the closest relatives.

The assistant professor, finding a topic that stimulated and interested him, enrapturedly continued in a heightened tone, as if facing a broad auditorium of listeners: "In that precise period when a person is swollen from hunger, everything dies within that was attained

14

through culture and upbringing, and all familial feelings die. In their place appear with ardent force the primal instincts of a hungry animal, an animal that suffers pangs of hunger and forcefully grabs food from the mouths of weaker beasts, even though this weaker animal might be its child, spouse, or mother. Then all of the precious emotions accumulated over centuries of civilization disappear, and the bloated human becomes only a hungry beast."

Katrusia listened to the assistant professor, swallowing hungry saliva, and recalled her neighbor, engineer Hryhory, who died from hunger last week and who, being in a bloated state, grabbed food from his five-year-old son. Hryhory unquestionably was a civilized person who loved his only son Yurchyk immeasurably.

"In men," as if replying to Katrusia's thoughts, the assistant professor continued, "these reactions are more violent than in women, because men react to hunger's pain more acutely. The statistics of those dying from starvation, which I am now analyzing, show that the percentage of men who die from hunger is significantly greater than of women."

The two had long ago passed the ice-covered section of Pushkin Street and neared the turnoff to Lermontov, where Katrusia lived. They were met by a sleigh with another corpse, which pulled out of a courtyard, a sleigh pulled by a girl of about fourteen, who was harnessed to the sleigh from the front. This young girl certainly had friends or neighbors, but nobody helped her, and this was completely normal.

Hungry people lose all normal feelings, and in this situation, obviously, sympathy for the troubles of others. Every hungry person attempts to conserve the remnants of their energy at all costs, and understandably in these times, no one accompanies a good friend to the cemetery; no one will help the widow or the orphan in their woes.

For Katrusia, the cruel facts of contemporary life were now becoming evident, filled with simple, and at the same time, tragic, content.

Assistant Professor Vsevolod almost did not notice the new death. Engrossed, he continued to speak, holding Katrusia with his right hand while waving his left in the air. His coat collar opened, revealing a scrawny neck full of veins, and his fur hat slid back, displaying an academic's high forehead and temples covered with gray.

"First of all, you're risking a chill," Katrusia said, peeking at the assistant professor with a quick eye. "Secondly, it is nearing four o'clock, and you have probably forgotten that you have the misfortune to live in a city where there are no trams, no cars and no coachmen, and that you live on the other side of Kharkiv. Therefore, you risk being shot by the German crossing guards for being out at a forbidden time. Who then will finish the scientific work about hunger's influence on the human psyche? Thirdly, take your hand, because I have arrived home and must bid you adieu."

The assistant professor with an obvious curiosity looked at his hand which, in helping Katrusia to cross the ice spot, he had simply forgotten to retrieve. Raising his eyebrows, he asked with his gaze: "By what manner could my right hand have ended up there?" Nevertheless, he slowly and deliberately took the hand back.

Katrusia's laughter had a ring to it. "Your forgetfulness grows with every step," she said. "I fear that when you become an old, renowned scholar, your absentmindedness will reach anecdotal proportions. I fear also that, while working on the hunger problem, you definitely do not notice that you yourself starve. You have lost a lot of weight lately. Why is that? With your immense medical practice, you do not have to be hungry!"

These final words to the academic Katrusia pronounced with a sympathetic note.

"You know very well, Katrusia, that I treat the starving for free; they cannot pay me with food, while money — what can you buy with money, these days?"

"And the Germans?" pestered Katrusia. "You heal Germans, and in that number, even German officers! For curing them, you get paid, again, not with money, but with food."

"The Germans, you say — German officers. At the beginning of treatment, like a law, they promise to pay, with bacon and chocolate, but when they are healthy or almost cured, they suddenly disappear forever."

"Well, certainly, now you are thinking only of your research, and you completely forget that from your patients, the Germans, you should demand payment for treatment in advance, or else partly in advance."

Katrusia was getting ready to give the academic a whole list of practical advice, but looking at the watch on her wrist, she almost died; it was half past three! How could the scatterbrained academic get home in time? "I beg you, please; run home quickly, or else the German patrols will shoot you!"

The assistant professor tightly squeezed Katrusia's hand and truly ran. Katrusia stood by the door of her dwelling and watched him, until his somewhat clumsy figure disappeared around the Pushkin street corner.

Early February, 1942.... It is only seven o'clock in the evening, yet Kharkiv drowns in darkness.... The streets are without

18

pedestrians, the windows of the buildings without light.... Especially frightening, in the background, drowning in the city's deep darkness, as reminders of recently-lived terrors, stand countless ruins of formerly large inhabited buildings.... Here is the dead mass of the Project Building burnt by the Soviets, there the terrible ruins of the NKVD district office, also burnt before the retreat.... Frightening ruins and still more frightening memories.... The buildings bombed by the Germans....The Southern Train Station and Post Office.... The wrecked railroad tracks and remnants of blown-up bridges, all vividly proclaim the absence of any contact whatsoever between the big city and the rest of the world....

Here is the center of Kharkiv, completely destroyed by the German bombardment and resulting fires.... It eloquently underlines, with giant piles of rocks, concrete and glass, that the metropolis no longer has a center.... It was destroyed by the ruinous storm of recent events, as were the water system, electricity generating station, the bridges, rail lines, train stations, tramway system, telegraph, telephone, post office.... Even the extra food supplies....

The large city without a center, what an insignificant thing it becomes.... The large city without fuel, without water, without food.... And even without any means of transport to

19

bring them in, because for the civilian population, there is no contact with the rest of the world.... The large city, which before the war had more than eight hundred thousand inhabitants, has now only three hundred thousand, and these are every day dying....

Oh, today in this city nobody is being born; they only die very intensely.... And where did the other five hundred thousand people go?... Three hundred thousand were evacuated by the Soviets, and the rest scattered on foot from this hell-city to neighboring towns and villages, or died of hunger in the three and a half months that passed from the moment of German entry into Kharkiv, a memorable date for all Kharkivites — October 24, 1941!... The food supplies were evacuated by the Soviets, and what wasn't shipped was destroyed by government decree, in most cases burnt, or otherwise rendered unfit for consumption....

The large, dying city now becomes a city on the front, because the front line stubbornly sticks for a long time not far from it, along the banks of the Donets River.... This makes it harder to make contact with nearby districts.... It becomes a giant military center....

Oh, how many armed people there are here, that walk in green-blue uniforms and converse in a language incomprehensible to most people!... Entire army regiments come to the large city from the front, to rest.... They look for amusement, and young female bodies.... And these they find easily, because they can pay, with bread, food....

Large convoys of wounded from the front come to the large city for healing; they lie in hospitals, and while they are seriously ill, seek nothing.... But when they are somewhat healthier, they also will seek amusement and women's bodies.... They also will find them....

In the city there is a network of permanent German establishments: command centers, police stations, supply organizations, mess halls, barracks, and also a complete line of various others, labeled ABTEILUNG and SHTAFFEL, the activities of which for the population remain a mystery.... The workers in these numerous establishments also search for amusement and women's bodies.... And, understandably, also find them; the more so, because this army category belongs to Kharkiv's so-called permanent population: they occupy their quarters and settle down comfortably, in all meanings of the word....

It would be a crime against armed people in green-blue uniforms to say that they only seek amusement and young female flesh.... In order to be objective, one has to justly note that, in their searches, there is something more serious, a functional order, and that all of them without exception seek to profitably buy gold, diamonds, furs.... They seek and also find, because everything gravitates toward them; they have many mighty partners: hunger, foul weather and cold.... Even Nature, in the person of Frost the Joker, this year drives the water to the German mill....

This winter Frost allows himself overly brutal jokes; he sends the temperature of the winter air to unnaturally low levels, and with the fuel shortages makes hungry people incapable of the struggle to survive.... The numerous army of speculators from the local population systematically assists the Germans to amass gold from the hands of a hungry and cold people croaking in unheard-of woes....

The Germans seek female flesh and gold, usually at night.... At four o'clock in the afternoon, just as the curfew approaches, on a large city's empty streets, drowned in darkness, one will meet only armed people in green-blue uniforms.... They walk alone, or in small groups of two or three, and in the quiet of the frost-filled air, from afar can be heard their heavy steps on the creaking snow....

Along Pushkin Street, where the wind is having fun sweeping the snow, uncovering an icy spot, walk two soldiers in green-blue uniforms.... One of them suddenly slips and almost falls, but remains on his feet....

Blurting, "Donnerwetter," he walks further, gaily talking with his companion....

On the corner of Basin, they come to a guard post.... There is a short exchange of words, a password spoken, and again they go on.... Passing Lermontov not far from Pushkin Cemetery, they stop; lighting a pocket lamp, they carefully look for the number of a small building; finding it to be the right one, they go to the door.... For a moment the lamp lights up their epaulets with the brilliant officers' insignia.... Why do they come here?... What do they seek?... Young girls, or inexpensive gold?...

Oh, the great half-ruined city that drowns in darkness only appears dead!... Don't believe that it is stuck in dead men's inertia!... Don't believe its dark, lifeless windows!... Behind these dark windows people still live, someplace.... People, who haven't died yet, and who do not want to die.... People, who at all costs want to appease their animalistic hunger and warm their tortured bodies, tortured with everlasting cold.... People, who in suffering follow a tragic path, losing the feelings accumulated over centuries of civilization.... People, who create for themselves a new morality that justifies every evil deed, and which can be proclaimed with these few words: "Everything is good which allows me the opportunity not to die of hunger...."

Those who travel on this path survive, and some even become rich; those who protest and waver and try to avoid this new 'morality' systematically die, providing Assistant Professor Vsevolod rich material for his hunger problem study.... For the research subject is: 'How Hunger Influences the Human Psyche....'

Katrusia's dark braids circled her head like a crown; she had serious dark eyes beneath black semicircle brows, the same brows which her friends described as 'string-like.' Katrusia had a smooth cheek, a pleasant smile and straight little teeth. But she had a completely pale, tired face without any trace of color. The small, once-enticing figure, once so neat, had by now became scrawny and flat, like a board. Still, recently, only two or three months ago, Katrusia brought attention to herself with her looks. Now... now one had to gaze carefully at her to say that she was once beautiful and that maybe she still could be, if only she would eat.

"Yes, yes," Katrusia said to herself, looking at her reflection in the mirror that stood on the table, lit by a miserly light from an oil lamp. Spontaneously, she was reminded of the Margarita aria from the opera *Faust*: "No, this is not you, Margarita. No, this is not you!"

The difference was that for Margarita the wonder was to notice the strange blossoming of her beauty, decorated with expensive ornaments, while for Katrusia it was the opposite, a premature loss of it.

"Yes, yes," Katrusia said to herself. "My friend Halya was perfectly correct when she told me that after two or three months of this starvation, it would be a fright to look at me. This has happened."

Katrusia stood up from the table, lit a fire in the iron stove and began to warm yesterday's beet soup, using little wood splinters for fuel. On her forehead a deep perpendicular wrinkle had set in, one which normally appeared only during moments of intensive thinking.

It was a small, clean room, but just as cold inside as out, the difference being that the wind did not twirl the snow indoors. In a corner were a few lengths of kindling that were further split into minute portions, and which were used only for cooking the beet soup which had by now become Katrusia's only daily meal, and which very soon would be no more.

One beet cost forty to fifty rubles in the bazaar. Where could she obtain such money when all her best dresses were sold long ago? Her bed linen was gone, and all her shoes, except those she wore. Sold, for almost nothing, and all spent on beets for the daily soup.

Katrusia slurped the hot stock in which finely-cut pieces of beet swam. Her young teeth greedily grabbed the beet pieces and minced them finely, with an outraged hunger for other food, one which could be bitten, gnawed, chewed, squeezing the invigorating tasty juice. She ate the beet stock, and wild fantasy painted Katrusia a piece of bread. Through the force of her will, she drove the tempting mirage away, while her mouth was overfilled with cold saliva and her teeth by themselves made the chewing motion. Bread! Katrusia had not eaten bread for over two months! It cost two hundred and fifty rubles a kilo!

Katrusia washed her little dish, turned off the oil lamp and lay down to sleep in her warmest dress, piling on top of herself a blanket, a comforter, and her winter coat.

Katrusia did not sleep; it was too cold. Secondly, thoughts do not allow sleep. Katrusia wanted to live. Oh, she now so earnestly wanted life, like she had never wanted before. Now, before death from starvation leered into her eyes, she had as a witness appraised the immense value that life has. Katrusia wanted to live, and because of that she examined the last three and a half months with a critical eye.

She certainly had made near-fatal mistakes that had allowed her to sink to such an emaciated state. Soon the stage of bloating would begin, and then maybe it would be too late to save herself. It was necessary to study her past three and a half months. However, through the prism of the past, our mistakes always become more understood. So said her late father, university professor and close friend of the strange Assistant Professor Vsevolod.

Two weeks before the German entrance into Kharkiv, Katrusia's husband Vasyl, who had been working as an engineer for two years, was mobilized to dig trenches. Vasyl never knew where exactly he was supposed to dig those trenches because, at that time, there were indeed trucks full of men mobilized to dig trenches, but only the authorities knew where they were being shipped.

Vasyl promised that at the first opportunity he would return home; he strictly commanded Katrusia to take care of herself at all costs and made her promise that during his absence, she would not destroy their first child. "Give me your word that you will not destroy our child!" he had said, even though Katrusia's pregnancy was only one month in term.

Katrusia gave her word. She was only twenty-two years old and she viewed this issue less seriously than Vasyl. She tried to convince him of the wartime hardships, and of her desire to finish university. She was a third-level student in the faculty of literature, and though military events had terminated studies at the university, Katrusia was determined that at the

27

first opportunity she would return and complete her program. All this did not influence Vasyl in the least. He was unmoved; he stood firm, and he was so happy that Katrusia was pregnant, and Katrusia gave her word.

Foreseeing hardships with food supplies, Vasyl and Katrusia made a stockpile: some flour, potatoes, buckwheat, oil and kindling. According to their calculations, it appeared that Katrusia had a safe food supply for two months, and Vasyl was convinced that within a month he would be home, and together they would somehow make do.

Some time after the German entrance, the men mobilized by the Soviets for trench-digging began to return. They stole home on foot, with great hardship, fighting hunger and cold all the way. Those who did not return from the trench-digging were also many, because even among her acquaintances Katrusia counted a number. She questioned the survivors about Vasyl, but they said that during the Soviet retreat there was great panic and such a crowding of people that it was hard to maintain contact with anyone. No, they had not seen Vasyl.

But Katrusia anxiously expected him daily, and when he didn't come today, then maybe he would come tomorrow. But days passed after days, which with mathematical mercilessness grouped into weeks and months, and Vasyl had not returned. Maybe he was killed during the bombing of the trenches, or maybe he had fallen into German captivity. This last thought left a crumb of hope for Katrusia's soul, because she had heard that the civilians who dug the trenches were receiving amnesty.

Her food supply, with great conservation, lasted two and a half months, and she was still cooking with the remnants of the kindling prepared by Vasyl. From the day Vasyl left, four months had passed. Four months ago it was possible to say with certainty that with the front nearing, a consequential shortage would come, which would last for a while, but no one, it seems, not even in their fantasies, thought that Kharkiv would for an undetermined time be a starving, dying island isolated from the rest of the world.

Katrusia in her youth had studied the French and German languages, but with the German she for some reason was lazy and over the years forgot it. Now this lack prevented her to some extent from obtaining work at a German establishment. At this time, the most lucrative positions were as dishwashers and waitresses at the German eateries, because this gave the workers the opportunity to eat well.

Educated, intelligent women competed with one another to obtain the selfish position of dishwasher in a German dining room. Other

29

positions in the municipal administration or in Kharkiv's civilian establishments paid very miserly wages — five hundred to seven hundred rubles a month, which could buy only three kilos of bread. For three kilos of bread, a person had to work one whole month, and the huge question "What to eat?" remained unanswered, and everyone decided for themselves, as they knew.

For the first while, Katrusia, having a food supply, consciously prevented herself from seeking a job; she wasn't so hungry, and was full of hope that soon, soon, Vasyl would return. To work as a dishwasher for the Germans — no! She would embark on that road only in the most extreme situation. But now, for the foreseeable future, this extreme situation did not seem improbable, and she started to renew her knowledge of German; in this area, Katrusia had substantial success.

During the first two months of German occupation, while Katrusia still had enough food and still looked like a very interesting young woman, there was no shortage of opportunities to become a German's lover; in fact, such propositions crossed her every step; they seemed to stick to her. But Katrusia high-handedly and stridently threw them all away.

That shameful possibility was locked away from her; a single thought about it filled her soul with disgust. Did she, a Ukrainian woman living in Ukraine, in order not to die from hunger, have to become a German soldier's lover who would be paid for her body with a piece of stolen Ukrainian bread?

How, and with what kind of eyes could she again meet Vasyl, who was the dearest person in the world to her? From the moment Vasyl departed, she felt that she did not remain whole, but only the smaller part; the bigger half, Vasyl, was forcefully amputated from her, and the place where the amputation took place now bled and painfully ached every day.

Through all of this she kept her word, and was still pregnant. Days passed after days and came together with mathematical orderliness into weeks and months. Four months of her pregnancy had passed. Soon, very soon, when four and a half months ended, she would feel the child's movement, his first movement. Katrusia was convinced that she would give birth to a boy, and even came up with a name for him: Tarasyk. Soon, soon she would feel Tarasyk's first movement.

It had been a month and a half since she had first felt really hungry, and the last two weeks she had suffered true hunger pangs. Obviously Tarasyk was also hungry, and because of this, her pain and suffering from hunger became still more acute and searing.

Katrusia, swallowing cold saliva, turned over onto her other side and tried to fall asleep. How could she fall asleep! Observing with a critical eye her past four months, Katrusia knew which mistakes she had made, what in her behavior had been erroneous, faulty. But her father had always said that one's mistakes become understandable only when they are past.

Maybe Katrusia should have had an abortion and broken her promise to Vasyl. Assistant Professor Vsevolod, her father's former associate and a trusted family friend, certainly would have helped her in this. He would have spoken himself with an appropriate gynecologist, and for her, certainly, they would have performed the abortion carefully, professionally, and without cost. But from this thought, Katrusia shuddered with her whole body, and her soul filled with a new passion for Tarasyk, a passion new to her which she could not describe in words, because language is too poor for this. "No, no!" Determined and convinced, Katrusia whispered to herself: "It is perfectly justified that I did not have an abortion, just as it is justified that I did not become a German's lover."

However, Vasyl was not there, and at all costs it was necessary to save the child and herself. Obviously, the extreme time would come for her, which would force her to become a German dishwasher or waitress. This would still be better than being a German's lover.

Katrusia's thoughts spun further and she reminded herself that her friend Halya lived with an old German who worked in the supply division. Halya long ago fruitlessly tried to convince Katrusia that in order to save her life, she definitely had to become a German's lover. Halya was a good woman and Katrusia's true friend from school days; because of this, she never stopped giving Katrusia what she considered to be good advice.

Meeting Katrusia a few days before on the street, Halya was shocked at Katrusia's appearance. She cursed her as only she could "for her stupid stubbornness," and finally, thinking for a moment and remembering something, she said to Katrusia, "My German lover Fritz told me yesterday, that with his involvement, a new officers' mess is being organized and there will be a selection process for the female serving personnel. Therefore, Katrusia, if this interests you, I can speak to Fritz about it."

Katrusia thanked Halya for her kindness and said that she would think about it.

Now, recollecting this meeting with Halya, Katrusia decided to go next morning to Halya and ask for her protection before Fritz. She understood the most commonly-used German words and she could certainly handle the waitresses' uncomplicated conversations. Relieved at having arrived at this decision, she finally fell asleep.

Halya, a woman of twenty-six years with a luxurious hairdo of ringlets, a meaty, snubbed nose, full cheeks and minute teeth similar to those of a mouse, peered pointedly from above brightly-painted lips when she smiled.

Halya knew that her face was plain, banal, maybe even vulgar. From this perspective, she did nor create any illusions for herself; nobody would paint a Madonna using her face, as she liked to say about herself, but this was totally inconsequential for her. Halya believed that her main weapon was her luxurious body, which she always and very conscientiously cared for.

For Halya to lose weight was a horrific proposition which filled her primitive soul with a beastly fear. Because of this, Halya became acquainted with 'Herr Fritz' who worked in the supply division, and very quickly became his lover. Being Fritz's lover, she not only had enough bread, but also the opportunity to obtain other things like sausage, butter and sugar. And this would provide the opportunity to retain her luxurious body. Among other things, Halya had a husband who was someplace on the front, but this did not prevent her from being Fritz's lover.

As children long ago, Katrusia and Halya went to school together, studied in the same classroom, sat together on the same bench. Katrusia studied very diligently and helped Halya in her studies. Halya, who was over-age, was the oldest girl in her class and always distressed the teachers with the limits of her mental capabilities. Katrusia became the protector of the mentally-limited Halya, and it seems if it weren't for Katrusia's guardianship, Halya may never have finished school.

At present, however, the mentally-limited and physically-sated Halya was ready to take under her protection the hungry and impoverished Katrusia. Now knowledge, talents and intellectual development were not valuable; now not even a pretty face and 'string-like' eyebrows were valuable. Now a new morality ruled, with a new outlook on life and people.

Halya met Katrusia very happily, kissing her on both cheeks, taking off her coat which hung on her emaciated figure as if on a board, and immediately seated her by the table.

It was pleasant in Fritz's house and very warm, and on the table Katrusia saw German bread. Real bread, and — the wonder! — sausage and butter! Katrusia had not seen such things for a very long time, and even her imagination did not paint them. Her eyes involuntarily welded themselves to the food on the table; in her throat was a spasm and her mouth filled with saliva.

With great exertion, she wrestled her eyes from the food and hoarsely proclaimed, "I, Halya,... came to you...."

"It is marvelous that you did come, because I have two important propositions for you. And if you had not come to me today, then I would have had to run to you to your Lermontov Street. But first sit, Katrusia, and eat."

Halya poured Katrusia coffee with milk, cut off a slice of bread, buttered it, and on top of it placed a piece of rosy sausage, in which glistened alluring pearls of fat.

Katrusia ate, forgetting about the goal of her visit to Halya, forgetting even about Halya herself. She was completely incapable of directing her movements, of making them less jagged in the process of consuming food. She ate greedily, as a starving person eats. Her young teeth did not succeed in chewing, because she prematurely swallowed that which was not chewed. The passionate softness of the sausage and the healthy affections of the butter filled her being with such satisfaction that she shuddered involuntarily with her whole body.

Halya sat and looked over Katrusia with an unmasked curiosity. Her serious gaze stopped on Katrusia's emaciated boardlike state. When Katrusia had finished eating, Halya silently stood up and poured her a second cup of coffee, buttered a second slice of bread, covered it with sausage and again sat down to observe.

This second portion Katrusia ate more slowly and with more restraint; she now was able to control her movements and shamedly peered at Halya. It was very embarrassing for her, that outburst of uncontrolled hungry gorging in front of her friend's eyes, and she understood that she was the object of Halya's observations. Both were silent. Finally, when the second portion was eaten, Halya spoke. She felt herself to be mistress, and she now had the word, while Katrusia was supposed to listen to her.

"First of all, tell me, where is your bust?" said Halya, soberly examining the spot where Katrusia's bust was supposed to be.

Not getting any reply, she continued in the same manner: "Have you realized, you worrying and dreaming soul, that you have lost all signs of womanhood, that your face looks more like a death mask than the face of a young lady? Have you realized that you no longer have a body, just a skeleton? And only in his name, in order to protect a faithfulness to a Vasyl who no one needs, who may never return!"

Halya paused, a pause which had many meanings, obviously waiting for an answer, but Katrusia sat silently, small, cowering, emaciated. Under the influence of the warmth in Halya's room, and the hot healthy food, her whole tortured being softened, melted and drifted toward sleep, while Halya's bellicose tirades she heard as if through some sort of thick wall, as if from afar.

All the while Halya continued: "Do you think, Katrusia, that I do not know what a deep difference always existed between us? When we finished school together, you were a seventeen-year-old beauty with a Madonna's face and your figure was so beautifully defined that men always looked at you on the street, and long after watched you in the distance. Do you remember yourself that day, finishing school in a light, bright dress and in a great straw hat, with knee-length black braids? Oh, I remember you well! You yourself at that time did not understand how fantastically beautiful you were; you did not know your own quality. But I knew your worth; at that time I was twenty-one and a well-corrupted girl with a crooked, vulgar mug and a luxurious body.

"It was usually very unpleasant to walk down the street with you or ride the trams, because all the men fastened their lustful gazes on you; and you alone, you saintly simpleton, did not see this, and if you saw it, did not understand it. Added to all this, you were talented, mentally grown-up, intellectual, full of all sorts of dreams of life. Every teacher in our school considered you smart and me a deadhead, even completely stupid. Now look at you and look at me. In life's difficult circumstances, when the majority of the population is dying of hunger, I live in plenty and warmth and eat the very best. I even buy wonderful items for myself, oh, so cheaply, for a slice of bread. I buy gold for Fritz and in this profit well for myself. And you have sunk to the status of skeleton! You with your figure did not know how to find yourself a lover who would save you from a starving death. If I had your exterior, I would have hooked a general! Well, after all this, tell me, which one of us is stupid, and who is smart?"

Such a comparison was personally pleasing for Halya. Wasn't this the triumph of self-satisfaction over dreamy idealism? The triumph of vulgar primitiveness over the highly-developed intellect? Halya's greenish little eyes narrowed and flashed an evil flame, the flame of personal self-satisfaction. She looked at Katrusia, waiting for an answer, but there was no answer. Putting her head and hands on the table, Katrusia quietly cried. There was something sorrowful, painful in those quiet tears, in those bent, thin, sharpened shoulders. Something suddenly angered Halya and reminded her that she had strayed from her theme, because her speech's original idea had been how to aid Katrusia in poverty.

"Don't worry, Katrusia," she said. "Wipe your tears and listen carefully to me. I have two propositions for you. The first: a respected old German is looking for a proper wife for himself. He especially wants one who is young, intelligent and proper. All these qualities you possess. The trouble is that you are so hideously thin."

Halya was lost in thought for a moment, and then said: "I'll tell him that you're a weird one, that you have yet to live with a German, and because of that, you starved and lost weight. Maybe this will make him more desirous. Because, you may as well know, Katrusia, he is already taken with you! I showed him your photograph and you pleased him. He asked me to come to an agreement with you."

"Leave it, Halya. Your first proposition does not suit me," answered Katrusia, looking directly into Halya's eyes. "What does your second proposition entail?"

"I beg you, Katrusia, explain to poor, stupid me why you are so stubbornly rejecting it. Is it only in the name of faithfulness to Vasyl that you prefer to die in great suffering and at twenty-two enter the earth? You, with your figure, with your talents, with your education! Do you not pity yourself?"

"Listen, Halya, as a Ukrainian, I do not wish to sell my body to a German who will pay me with food stolen from my own Ukraine. I know that you cannot understand this, but you really do have a good heart, and if not with your mind, then maybe with your woman's heart you can understand the other reasons. I will tell you in a few short words, but you must hear me through. From what I say you will understand me, or if you do not, never mention it to me again."

"The first reason, Katrusia, is your high idealism, which I do not acknowledge, and which I even condemn. But I am listening. Tell me your other reasons, and I swear I will never reproach you again for them."

"Well, firstly, I love Vasyl and can never betray him. Secondly, I'm... pregnant... already four months, from the beginning of October."

"You, pregnant?" Halya whispered, and then she became numbly quiet. She was completely stunned by this revelation. "You, pregnant? Dear God, with what do these flighty idealists think? Certainly not with their heads!"

Halya still more intently examined Katrusia's emaciated figure for a moment and added: "You can't even imagine what kind of stupidity you are doing! Who gives birth now? Probably in the whole of Kharkiv, you are the only such 'smart' person left... you...."

"Enough, Halya. Be quiet now. You promised me that you would not pressure me any more

41

with your questions. Please give me your second proposition."

"Very well. The other proposition is significantly worse than the first, and it seems that it is somewhat known to you," Halya continued in a quieter manner. "My Fritz is currently involved in the work tied to the opening of an officers' mess. Well, I talked with Fritz and he promised to put you in. At eight tomorrow morning you have to be at the building. I will write the address down for you. Tomorrow a group of women will wash the floors and organize the mess building, and from this group, a smaller number will be selected as permanent workers for the mess, as dishwashers and waitresses."

"Good, Halya, I accept. Tell your Fritz that I will be there tomorrow. You say that we will wash floors and decorate the building?"

"Yes, this is done after renovations. It is dirty work which your delicate hands are not quite used to," Halya explained dryly, from the shadow of her anger.

"Hard, dirty work doesn't frighten me. Thank you Halya, for the treats and for this second proposition," Katrusia said, getting dressed. Suddenly, she wanted to leave Halya immediately; now, now, away! In point of fact, Halya no longer detained her. "Good bye, Halya," she said. "And thank you."

"Good bye, Katrusia. It was nothing."

The following morning, Katrusia arose at seven, more determined and more enthusiastic than normal; today she would go to work, would wash floors and walls, and decorate the filthy building which was to house the German officers' mess.

"What to wear?" flashed in her head, but she untangled this question in half a minute. Definitely, it was necessary to wear something old, something worn, that would not matter if it were spoiled with dirty work. She put on a worn dress with elbow patches, thick woolen stockings and old sports shoes with low heels, and a warm old kerchief. She felt she had to guard against the frost and cold; she couldn't get chilled and become sick now that she was pregnant. In this endeavor, she felt her looks to be quite unimportant; the important thing was to be warm, and ready for dirty work.

Katrusia quickly ran down the street, with the frost painfully pinching the toes on her feet, and her small body shivered; she hadn't eaten anything, but she was full of hope, hope that today she would be fed by the Germans. Katrusia was running to wash their filthy floor for them after the renovations.

She arrived at the building just on time, precisely at eight o'clock. The large entrance doors opened with a shy push, and she found herself in a large, chilly vestibule, where she joined a mass of young women and girls. The day lit the vestibule with a miserly light; it passed with difficulty through the multicolored, frozen window panes, and Katrusia, coming in from the street, was not immediately comfortable in her new surroundings.

In the first moment, the only thing that struck her was the women's shrill, ringing, youthful laughter. The mass of women buzzed like a hive of frightened bees. Katrusia's appearance in the vestibule did not draw any attention, and she leaned with her back against the wall, silently observing the proceedings. It all looked very strange and confusing to Katrusia. The women were changing clothes, making themselves up.

Almost everyone had a small valise containing elegant shoes and thin spider-web stockings. Galoshes, felt boots, old clumsy shoes, thick woolen stockings; all these were removed and stuffed into the valises. In their place, the women's legs were, with quick movements in the cold room, clad with other, more elegant coverings: colored spider-web stockings and high-heeled shoes. Under their coats, almost everyone had a short, elegant dress, often with a low neckline. If beneath the coat there was a heavy sweater, it was also placed in the valise. The women's heads were bare, and almost every head had a hairdresser's precise style. One held a small pocket mirror for the other, and everyone brought into order the fake curls crushed by the fabric of their now-removed scarves and hats. With the odd exception, these were all young girls aged about twenty and younger; some were markedly thin from hunger, while a few still looked fairly healthy.

"Maybe there's to be a ball here, and Halya gave me the wrong address," Katrusia thought, confused by the show. Leaning against the wall not far from the entrance doors, she looked about her. "But a ball at eight in the morning? This also is improbable. Maybe it's a German holiday today, and because of that, a ball?"

For Katrusia one thing was clear. She had stumbled into the wrong place; it was impossible that girls dressed in ball gowns would come to wash floors.

Katrusia was about to leave when a woman approached her, age twenty-eight, modest, combed and dressed normally, not ready for a ball. "The two of us here are the eldest," she said laughing, "but forgive me for the word. Say rather, more stupid than the rest. Completely green youth understands the situation, while we, the elders, do not."

Katrusia did not know what to reply to this. Silent for a moment, she finally asked the other woman, "Please tell me, why have you come to this place?"

"I came to wash floors. I am a teacher, but now I am starving terribly with a child and would be happy to become a dishwasher in a German cafeteria."

Katrusia looked closely at the teacher's face; beneath her eyes there were puffed-up semicircles, an unmistakable mark of an extreme stage of starvation. "Well, what did these girls come here for?" asked Katrusia.

"These girls, the majority of whom were selected and sent here by the Director of the Women's Labor Bureau, have also come here to wash floors."

On this the conversation ended, as Halya's lover, Fritz, entered the vestibule. Katrusia had seen him twice, the last time a month ago, and recognized him immediately. He was a tall, massively-built German, about fifty years of age, with a red almost blown-up face and gold teeth. These gold teeth had been installed in Kharkiv; when Katrusia saw him for the first time in December, he did not have gold teeth. This detail immediately threw itself into Katrusia's eyes when Fritz opened his mouth to speak. "Guten morgen," he said to the mass of women. The women, in stammering their replies to the greeting, first became agitated, then froze and quietened.

Fritz coughed and asked which women understood German well. A few voices squeaked "ich, ich," but no one came forward. Fritz waited, and the teacher stepped up to him and told him that she could help him communicate with the mass of women.

Fritz spoke and the teacher translated. After Fritz's directives, everyone entered the cafeteria site. The site consisted of two large, completely empty halls, very dirty and splattered with fresh lime and paint. But it was warm, as the building's central heating had been repaired. Fritz quickly looked over the women's documents; all the girls were truly sent by the Women's Labor Bureau's director. The teacher gave him a note which he read and stuffed into a pocket. Katrusia did not have anything. She approached Fritz quietly and said in German, "I am Katrin, Halya's friend."

"Ah, so, so," said Fritz, as if surprised. He looked at her miserable, poorly-dressed figure and said, "I did not recognize you."

Meanwhile, the elegantly dressed girls with the stylists' curls took off their coats, placed them on a paper in one corner of the hall, and stood in a row to receive Fritz's directions.

Fritz delegated some to clean windows and others to wash floors. What criteria he used in making this division was not known until the girls climbed onto the sills and stretched to scrape the lime and dirt off the glass. Katrusia noticed with interest that the youngest and best-looking girls ended up cleaning the windows. The second-rate girls, among them Katrusia and the teacher, were delegated to the washing of floors.

The work on the windows was relatively clean. They were not washed on the outside because they were frozen over, but the dirt was cleaned from the inside, on the glass, the sashes, and the sills. However, the floor washing was truly an uncommonly dirty job. But an order is an order. The girls of the floor detail hitched up their already too-short dresses and began to wash the floor, showing Fritz their legs with stretched, spider-web stockings of various fashions. The dirty water, mixed with lime, ran over the shiny toes of their elegant shoes, but the girls, as was evident, did not worry; they washed the floor gaily and joked among themselves, as if that was the way it was supposed to be.

Katrusia also washed the dirt and lime with the teacher, and with great curiosity awaited the next event. She was curious as to the reason for the costumes. Had all these girls dressed this way to conquer the attentions of the golden-toothed Fritz?

Tall, massive Fritz left briefly, then reappeared to supervise the girls' work. He did not hurry them, or yell at them in order to get the work done. Generally it was strange; why had the Women's Labor Bureau sent so many girls? There were at least twenty-five of them, maybe more. It seemed to Katrusia that to get the dining hall in order, four women would have been enough. Yet here there were amassed twenty-five; there was no order and Fritz did not have any desire to demand order.

But when the youngest girl of those working on the windows jumped down and said to Fritz that work on the windows was done, Fritz shouted at her, ordering her to climb up to the same window sill and clean it "noch einmal."

The girl was small and poorly-dressed, age about thirteen, with a very thin, pretty face with two large cheekbones. She had tried to do her work quickly and well, to earn the praise of the German authority. When the confused girl climbed back up to the window sill, her neighbor, a robust girl of eighteen said: "Don't be stupid; work slowly. Don't you see how everybody else works?" All the others worked slowly and lackadaisically. Katrusia herself worked slowly, anxiously waiting for lunch. With the slow and boring work, slowly and lackadaisically passed the minutes.

Suddenly a commotion was heard in the vestibule, along with loud German voices and laughter. Fritz, with unexpected lightness, jumped to the door and opened it with an expression on his face of great respect for his important guests. Several German officers appeared; two were fairly young and one was about fifty, obviously with a higher rank, as he entered first and marched straight ahead with the others trailing. Fritz respectfully brought up the rear.

The officers stopped near the windows and with interest examined the girls who stood on the window sills in short dresses and high-heeled shoes. Everyone's gaze was directed to the spot where the distinguished guests stared. This truly was not a bad showcase of women's legs which Fritz had masterfully selected. On the six window sills in the hall stood twelve pretty and very young girls. There were blondes, brunettes, red-heads. There was even a fairly robust one, unusual in starving Kharkiv. The others all had an average complexion and a tendency to thinness.

Here, wrapped in multicolored spider-web stockings, were various sizes and styles of women's legs, which on the high window sill pedestals under the bright rays of the February sun, could be satisfactorily observed. Oh, Fritz knew what he was doing when he put the best girls on the sill! Only the small poorly-dressed girl with the large cheekbones was a sad stain on this bright canvas. But even she had her own value; she was the bud of a future flower; she was a green strawberry, which still had a bitter taste.

The officers unceremoniously evaluated the goods in detail, examining the girls from head to foot, from foot to head, and exchanged amongst themselves pointed questions which brought from them friendly laughter.

They moved from one window sill to the next, evaluating, testing, joking, asking each girl her name and whether she knew German.

The oldest officer noticed the little girl, who stood on the last window sill with wide-open, childish eyes, fixedly staring at the officers.

"How are you to be called, little one?" he asked in German.

"Irene," the girl's thin answer echoed in the huge hall.

"Can you speak German?"

"Yes, sir. My mother taught me German."

"Ah! Do you have a mother, a father?"

"No sir; my father died a long time ago, while my mother died a week ago of hunger."

"Ah, so," the senior officer said to Irene. Turning to Fritz, he ordered: "Little Irene shall serve at my table." The oldest officer, it seemed, liked the bitter taste of unripe strawberries.

Katrusia well understood this conversation, and she was as engrossed in the proceedings as were the others.

The distinguished guests, having examined the girls on the window sills, then turned their enlightened attention to the girls of the second detail, who washed the floors. Once again, pointed German questions, jokes, and scattered laughter. Two fairly plump, well-built girls, rare in starving Kharkiv, drew the attention of the two younger officers, and it seemed to Katrusia that Fritz received a directive regarding these two girls.

Katrusia and the teacher washed the floors near the exit doors. The departing officers walked right by them, as if by an empty space.

At the end of the working day, when both halls were finally in order, Fritz announced the names of the women who were accepted for cafeteria work in the positions of dishwashers, kitchen help, and waitresses. There were twelve successful ones; ten of them were from those who had stood on the window sills and the others were the two robust girls who washed the floors and appealed to the young officers. The two most emaciated ones with the look of starving intellectuals, who had had the luck to stand on the window sill, did not make it to the cafeteria, because it is a known fact that the Germans really do not like thin people. It was not enough that the emaciated intellectuals spoke German fairly well, while the robust girls knew none at all.

Fritz explained that the girls would serve in the cafeteria during lunch and supper, and that they would spend the night in the same building, because being out at night was banned by the authorities. He added that the building was heated, and rooms for the girls had been arranged.

Katrusia and the teacher walked down the street. A hungry death stared both in the eyes, and they walked silently. "Pity the little girl!" said the teacher, finally.

"Yes," answered Katrusia.

They reached the corner and went their separate ways silently, crushed. "Till the next time, if we remain living."

Three days passed. Waking up in the morning and looking in the mirror, Katrusia saw barely-visible, puffy semi-circles beneath her eyes. Looking at her feet, she was stunned; her small ankles were no longer thin. They looked enticing, and even beautiful, just like they had been when she was not starving. On Katrusia's extremely thin skeleton, her feet began to improve and already looked almost normal. Cold sweat appeared on Katrusia's temples. There was no doubt; starvation bloating had started.

"How could I have not noticed this earlier?" whispered Katrusia with trembling lips. Quickly, nervously getting dressed, she thought: "Probably why I didn't feel my feet puffing up is because I am now wearing overly loose shoes. The starving, in the beginning of bloating, usually feel that their footwear becomes tight."

Where to run? To whom to turn? Where to look to be saved?

Later that same day, Katrusia waited by the office of Assistant Professor Vsevolod, until he finished administering to his patients. She had determined to discuss it with him, as with a doctor, and as her late father's friend.

It was twenty minutes after noon. All the doctors had finished their appointments and had gone off, who knows where, to look for something to placate the stomach's unceasing demands. Only Assistant Professor Vsevolod was in his office.

The polytechnical school's large corridors were empty; only the solitary Katrusia nervously awaited her old friend. She stood leaning against the office doors, involuntarily listening. From the office she heard the assistant professor's voice, well-known to her, which quietly said something, and a clear childish crying, sobbing.

Ten long minutes passed; suddenly the office doors flew open, and out ran a girl of sixteen with a childish, crying face and long, straw-colored braids tied at the ends with black ribbons. She had the look of a school girl, final year. She ran down the corridor to the exit, not even aware of Katrusia, who long and anxiously stared after her.

Meanwhile, the assistant professor came into the corridor, and with a broad smile on his lips gave Katrusia his hand. "I am so happy that you came! I was going to visit you today to see if everything is in order," he said, squeezing Katrusia's thin, bony fingers.

"What was this school girl doing in your office, and why was she crying?" asked Katrusia, forgetting about her own troubles for the moment.

"That, Katrusia, is a doctor's secret; there are thousands of such secrets on my mind, and because of this, they stop being secrets and become a true evil, about which one has to talk and about which it wouldn't hurt for a young woman like you to know," bitterly said Assistant Professor Vsevolod.

They went down a half-dark corridor, then down the stairs toward the exit. "She really is a school girl," continued the assistant professor. "She was infected with syphilis by a German officer. That is why she ended up in my office."

Exiting onto the street, where the February sun shone as if it were spring, the assistant professor carefully looked at Katrusia's face, and sharply changed the subject, speaking with a sincere worry in his voice: "Katrusia, you do not look well to me! It is not possible this way! I know everything, I understand everything. Oh I know you well! You are not one of those women who sell their bodies to the Germans, and because of that you starve. Do not contradict! You have the appearance of a seriously starving person, who is just about to start to bloat."

"You are mistaken," Katrusia said, barely keeping back the tears. "I am not just about to start to bloat, I am already bloating. This morning there were small semi-circles beneath my eyes and my feet already have improved, become normal, like they once were. On top of all this, I'm five months pregnant."

The assistant professor stopped and intently directed his horrified gaze at Katrusia's face. "Why did you not tell me about your pregnancy earlier?" he asked sternly and turned on the spot, heading back to the clinic.

"Where are you going? The road to your home is in the opposite direction! Oh, the absentmindedness of academic men!" Katrusia made an unsuccessful attempt at a joke.

"I am not going home, but to the clinic, because I have one more patient to see."

"I don't want to go," Katrusia said with tears in her voice, suddenly feeling disoriented and shamed, but obediently trudging after her old friend to the clinic.

56

He examined Katrusia carefully, in detail, extensively, touched her small swollen feet, and finally, firmly and somewhat angrily said: "The situation is serious, especially considering the pregnancy. But it is not hopeless, and together we will concentrate on saving you and the child. You certainly want a boy? Have you thought of a name yet?"

"Yes," Katrusia said quietly. "Tarasyk."

"Tarasyk, Tarasyk," repeated the assistant professor. "A good name. And the fact that Tarasyk is starving is not important to his mother! How could you not tell me earlier about your pregnancy?"

The assistant professor rifled through his cupboard, found something and locked the cabinet; then he rifled through his wallet, while Katrusia got dressed.

"Ready?" asked the assistant professor. "If you are ready, come here and listen to me carefully. Here are two bottles of gematogen, which you cannot get anywhere now. You know how to use it; certainly during childhood you drank it. Good. And here are one thousand rubles, with which you are today to go and buy yourself some food."

"I will take the gematogen," said Katrusia, "because that is medicine, but money I will not take, never." In her voice rang determination, insult and tears.

"It would be a miracle if Katrusia reacted differently. But you will take the money, and here is why: once when I was a young student and fell into poverty, your father saved me, giving me a substantial sum of money. Later, I came to pay my debt to your father but he did not want to take it. He said that he had enough money, and did not need it. Now you need it and the time has come for me to pay my debt. Write down what you must buy for yourself: a quarter-kilo of horse meat, there being no other available, onions, cabbage, carrots, and if possible, potatoes and flour. Eat often, but only a little at a time. Chew with your teeth a little piece of raw onion for a very long time. Eat the carrots and cabbage also raw; they are all vitamins. Combine small doses of meat with the starch of the potatoes and the vitamins."

The assistant professor gave Katrusia a list of instructions on how to revitalize herself, and also on how to behave. He spoke with a sincere, heart-like, fatherly tone; Katrusia was moved to tears and was forced to take the one thousand rubles, because the assistant professor placed them firmly into her bag. She silently took his large hand with both of hers and squeezed it.

"Do not allow hopelessness into your soul, and do not allow yourself ruinous thoughts. Remember, in the bloated stage, a person easily caves into feelings of carelessness, lies in bed and does not get up." Exiting into the street together with Katrusia, he said further: "I advise you, if you have the strength, to go to the bazaar today and secure a small food supply, because the question is, will you be able to walk to the bazaar tomorrow? You are in such a state that every day is crucial."

"I feel this," Katrusia said. "Today, in the morning, after seeing the first signs of swelling, I decided to sell or trade my only valuable possession for food. It is a ring with three diamonds. This, this family heirloom which was passed from generation to generation on the female side, from my great-grandmother to my grandmother to my mother, and from my mother to me. My mother commanded that I not sell it, that I take care of it and pass it on to my daughter-in-law. But today, in the morning, the fate of this family heirloom was sealed. I have to sell it, or better still, trade it. If I do not, I will never have a daughter-in-law."

"Yes Katrusia, save your life, or it will be too late. I know this ring; I saw it many a time on your late mother's hand. Just do not fall straightaway into the hands of some speculator, who will give you, hungry and impoverished, a few kilos of bread for it, like they usually do, while they themselves profit ten times over! First secure for yourself a week's supply of food, and only then prepare to sell your valuable slowly and carefully; do not hurry, whatever you do."

"It is only thanks to you that I have the opportunity to sell it slowly and carefully. I will not allow a speculator to profit from my need, from my hunger; I will not allow him to eat that kilogram of bread that rightfully belongs to me!" Katrusia cried angrily.

"Unfortunately, this is almost impossible, because the Germans buy everything they need, gold, diamonds, rarities, the best furs, only through speculators, and through them, they sell to us, swollen with hunger, our own Ukrainian bread, which was grown on our own land. Never in all my life have I seen such a gigantic army of speculators, which has propagated itself now, under the Germans, while our Ukrainian intelligentsia, Katrusia, and our workers die; already significant numbers of them have been wiped from the face of the earth. Each day carries new Ukrainian deaths to add to that number. Among others, yesterday Professor Petroshenko died of hunger. I also heard that during the past few days, the talented artist Shevchenko fell in the street; she never got up again."

"I knew her," Katrusia sadly answered.

"Prostitution and speculation; only these two shameful occupations provide the opportunity not only to survive, but even to prosper. Even intellectual occupations which are needed by the Germans, like doctors, starve to a greater or lesser extent, almost without exception. And what is there to say about the intellectual occupations not needed by the Germans, like our mathematicians, philosophers, Ukrainian writers, journalists?"

Just then they passed a jewellery store on Shumsky, in front of which stood a long line of people who filed into the side doors, while through the decorative front doors Germans entered the store. "Here, fancy this," contemptuously said the assistant professor. "Through the black side doors, gold from the hungry is accepted, while through the fancy front doors, it is sold to the sated Germans."

Katrusia passed the store, carefully looking at the faces of the impoverished people who were giving in their gold; tomorrow she would be waiting here.

"And now Katrusia, in order to entertain you somewhat, I'll tell you an anecdote from my personal life. I was going to work yesterday as usual, at eight in the morning. Suddenly a grimy soldier boy with a rifle approached me, pointed in my direction his dirty first finger and said, "Kom." I tried to explain to him in German that I was a doctor and was going to the clinic where sick people waited for me; in that group there were even Germans, but he didn't want to listen, mumbling something in his dialect and categorically repeating his order, "Kom!" Five minutes did not pass when in the same way he waved his finger at still another man, also telling him, "Kom!" In half an hour he had arrested twenty of us.

"We walked in front of him, wondering what would take place next. And he yelled at us, as if at animals with his dialect, and even cursing, so that we would walk faster. He led us in this manner to Moscow Street to a great pile of rock, sand and glass. As you yourself know, quite a bit is being knocked down following the bombardment, and he ordered us to clean up that pile. In other words, we had to load up slings and on our backs carry the debris to another place. Our protests did not accomplish anything, and the fact that I'm a doctor did not make any impression on him at all. I had to place my briefcase on the ground and get down to manual labor. Only at one o'clock in the afternoon was I relieved by a German with a higher rank who came to see if that pile of rubble had been moved.

"Do you think that he would apologize to me? I, an old Ukrainian intellectual, who from books had a completely different vision about German culture, stood and naïvely waited for him to apologize. I did not wait successfully; I finally went home. My patients also did not wait for me successfully that night. Interesting anecdote? A funny one?" asked the assistant professor and from his face and nervous hand movements, Katrusia saw that he was angered to the extreme.

Kharkiv's Central Blahovishchensky Bazaar, the so-called 'Blah Baz,' drones, screams, fidgets, lives a life that is too nervous.... This nervous intensity calls forth, it seems, an unheard-of disproportion between questions and propositions.... In the section of the bazaar where foodstuffs are sold, an unbelievably greater number of questions lord it over the propositions.... Thousands of hungry people mingle among the almost-empty tables with a burning desire to buy something to eat.... But there is nothing to buy.... From afar comes an old lady who carries something in a basket, and after her the whole mob runs.... The old one approaches a little table and begins to empty her basket, and all the hungry faces stretch in order to see, with the corner of one eye, what the old one has to sell.... Hands push one another in the most brutal fashion, in order to be the closest to the old lady who, feeling her importance before a hungry mob, slowly and solemnly brings out — oh, luxury! oh, luck! — raw potato peels.... The mob swirls, shouts, wavers, mutters....

Finally, with problems, a queue is created, at which point the physically stronger push the weaker out of the line.... Here, a tall obese woman pushes a small thin one out of the line and stands in her place.... The little one spins around and falls, but quickly stands up, and with a desperate determination shouts sharply, clearly, above the crowd's drone: "Oy, Baba!... Look around!... You are old and believe in God; help me!... I was pushed out of line and now I will not get any peels!..."

The old grandmother, the owner of a whole basket of potato peels, comes out determinedly in support of protecting the weaker's rights: "What are you doing, people?... Come to your senses!..." With dignity she speaks: "Have you become complete beasts?... I myself saw the little black-browed one.... Why did you push her out of the line?... Do you not have a crucifix, or what?... Let her back in, or I will sell no more!... I will go somewhere else with my goods!..." The crowd steps back and lets the small black-browed one back in to the queue....

"How much peel do you want, black-brow?..." the old lady asks her.... She spreads the peels out on the table in small piles.... Twenty rubles per pile.... The peels are wonderful; they are thickly cut, fresh, clean and have not been frozen.... The little black-browed one takes this into consideration, and feeling the baba's sympathy on her side, pleads: "Be so good Baba, give me two piles...."

"Do not give by twos, only one," roars the mob.... "Let there be some for all of us!..."

"I will give everybody one, but for this black-brow, I will give two!... My peels, my law!..." categorically states the old lady as she places two small piles into black-brow's basket and still pours in another handful....

"Oh, thank you, grandmother!..." says the black-browed one as she pays her forty rubles.... With difficulty she pushes her way through the crowd, sweaty, weakened, influenced by the scene she has just experienced, and stands by an empty table in order to rest.... The recently-conquered valuables, the potato peels, she wraps in paper so that they don't freeze and hides the packet at the very bottom of her basket.... She straightens her blue woolen hat which sits askew on her back, revealing black braids twice wrapped around her head.... She wipes the sweat from her face with a handkerchief and for a few moments stands motionless, with curiosity watching with what greed people grab the potato peels....

The little black-browed one was our acquaintance, Katrusia. Having acquired two piles of potato peels, she was clearly happy with herself. Washing them out, she can have potato soup twice! She rested and thought about the peels, and about the potatoes from which the peels were cut. She had often seen how Germans transport potatoes in automobiles. There was no doubt that these potatoes were grown in Ukrainian fields, and not far from Kharkiv in the nearby districts. But it was now only for the Germans. Nur für deutsche! And the population did not have enough peels. Such a valuable commodity as potato peels, only the girls who were lucky enough to work in the German dining hall could get, and only those who worked specifically in the kitchen, cleaning potatoes for the German dinner. In the process they cut the peels as thickly as possible and carried them home, for their mothers or sisters to sell in the bazaar. The baba in the market probably had a granddaughter working in a German kitchen.

"The grandmother is very old; she cannot have a young enough daughter who would have the opportunity to be placed in a German dining hall to work," Katrusia thought, reminding herself of her own failure. "If this grandmother had wanted, she could have charged more for the little pile. This is a good baba. May God save her."

Katrusia looked with her eyes, to see what else she could buy. Not far away, a woman stood selling millet in little glasses. She was probably the only one in the whole bazaar with such a luxurious commodity as millet. Because of this she asked eighty rubles per glass of millet, and people paid. If she had demanded one hundred rubles, they would still pay! True, there was not the crowd beside her as there was by the baba with the peels, but she was selling steadily and soon there would be no millet left.

Hungry, Katrusia imagined the taste of potato soup with millet, and her mouth filled with cold saliva. Her feet carried her by themselves to the lady with the millet; she bought one glass, amazing herself with her bravado, and — oh, terror! — paid eighty rubles! Then she went straight to the stall with bread and paid, for four hundred grams of bread, one hundred rubles. She hid the piece of bread as if it were the most precious jewel, and thought to herself: "May God prevent someone from pulling it out of my basket! Oh my, in one single day, I will spend all of the one thousand rubles my dear old friend gave me." Katrusia next bought a quarter-kilo of horse meat for thirty rubles and two large healthy beets at fifty rubles each.

Reminding herself that according to the advice of the assistant professor, she still had to buy cabbage, carrots and onion, and eat them raw, because these were the only vitamins now available, Katrusia walked through the whole bazaar, carefully searching for the needed vitamins, but they were not there. Walking among aisles of empty and half-empty tables, she saw large amounts of oil cakes which people were using instead of bread. She also saw flour made from acorns, which people bought and from which they baked something or cooked something. She saw rye, which sold by the glass for forty rubles each and oats for thirty rubles a glass and finally — oh, what luck! — she saw two onions. Like a hawk onto a chick, she threw herself onto these two onions and in a small voice asked, "How much?"

"Fifty for two," answered the trader. Katrusia paid, and smiling gratefully, hid the precious source of vitamins in her basket.

Finally she directed her steps homeward. Realizing how far it was to her home, Katrusia became terrified, frightened, weak. It seemed to her that she would not have the strength to return home, that she would not have the strength to cook for herself, that she would die in the bazaar with a full basket of expensive foods. What an evil, when in a large city there was no means of travel other than one's own feet! She stopped by an empty table in order to rest, and suddenly the thought of bread and onion filled her tired soul with hope. She peeled the smaller onion and broke off a small piece of bread, as per Assistant Professor Vsevolod's instructions, eating small portions. She chewed the bread and the juicy petals of onion with a feeling of sheer contentment, telling herself to eat slowly, not hurrying. At that moment, she saw nothing, heard nothing, forgot where she was; she just ate. Having eaten, she recovered herself, and selected the shortest path home.

In order to go in the desired direction, Katrusia cut across Tovkuchka, the second-hand market.

Tovkuchka is the spot in the bazaar where people sell their own items: clothing, footwear, domestic utensils.... Here too, rules a terrible disproportion between asking price and offer; naturally, the asking price dominates.... Here there are also thousands of hungry people, but in a different sense; here the sellers bring their items for sale and no one buys these things....

Aligning themselves in rows, these miserable people stand, shaking from the frost and cold, waiting fruitlessly whole days for a buyer.... They stand, displaying their dresses, coats, suits, footwear, standing stubbornly, because they are all unconquerable, they want to eat, they all suffer real hunger pains, and at the home of each waits a family, children, maybe already swollen from hunger.... They are parents with a burning desire for potato peels, or in extreme cases, for a piece of oil cake.... Here, often, for pennies magnificent items are given away and swift speculators take advantage of this situation....

Speculators, who spend whole days here, taking advantage of the most tragic situations for their own personal profit.... They exploit the greatest hellish pain in the world, hunger pain.... Like predators, they scurry about here, buying for the Germans items of interest, concentrating on gold, diamonds, rarities, furs, leathers.... In the bazaar, one never sees green-blue uniforms; the army prohibits it....

Looking at the bazaar superficially, one can obtain a completely false impression; one feels that the Germans do not squeeze the bazaar at all, as if the bazaar lives on its own, separated from German life.... It is necessary to enter the bazaar's inner life, dive into the denseness, in order to understand that this is not so.... That green-blue uniforms are not seen in the bazaar is true; however, for them, and in their interest, functions a huge army of jackals; speculators, maximizing, taking advantage of the hunger, cold and troubles of the population....

Katrusia crossed Tovkuchka directly, not stopping, because everything there was well-known to her; here she had sold her best items for pennies: beautiful shoes for two hundred rubles, less than a kilo of bread, a new fur coat for five hundred rubles, two kilos of bread, and many more similar items.

Now, as the gold market was on her way, she just wanted to pause there to determine the current price of gold.

Nearing Tovkuchka, she stopped to watch an interesting scene: a fat-faced dandy took a pitiful-looking older woman aside, a woman who carried contradictory signs of swelling on her face. From beneath his coat, he secretively showed her a loaf of German army bread and fervently spoke to her. However, the sight of the bread was a stronger influence on the woman than his flowery words, because she immediately gave the speculator a massive ring and took the bread, which with trembling hands she hid in her bag. The speculator, anxiously looking around, disappeared in the denseness of the gold market, and Katrusia approached the woman. "Excuse me," she said. "Can you tell me how much a gram of gold costs now?"

"I can," answered the woman. "For one gram of high-quality gold, speculators pay one hundred rubles."

"Thank you," said Katrusia and determinedly she walked away from the market. She was so exhausted with today's walking that she promised herself not to stop anywhere. The sooner home, the sooner to rest; her strength was drained to the extreme.

Taking herself away from the crowd, she was slowly walking on the bazaar's less-peopled stretches, making simple calculations: one gram of gold cost one hundred rubles, a kilo of bread cost two hundred and fifty rubles; therefore, one kilogram of bread equalled two and a half grams of high-quality gold.

The conclusion reached from this was disturbing. It meant that, having sold the ring, the family heirloom, she would delay the approach of a tragic end, death by starvation, by only a few days. "But the diamonds should be worth something," Katrusia said to herself, and this thought calmed her somewhat. In the meantime, she neared Christmas Street, and left behind the bazaar's life, noisy and full of inner tragedy.

On her right she saw a great crowd of people and wanted to avoid it, because bazaar and street events did not interest her. Probably a starving man stole a piece of bread from another starving man and now they grappled, or maybe somebody fell from malnutrition and was trying to recover on the bazaar's field; and people, always attracted to such scenes, stood and watched. Such scenes did not interest

Katrusia, and with a determined step she passed the crowd. She walked slowly so as not to fall, because it had cooled and the streets were very slippery.

Suddenly, something incomprehensible took place, frightful and striking, as if from the bright sky a bomb had been thrown. The crowd suddenly gasped and split into two uneven halves, freeing a great empty space, into which from above, from high up with a great force, pounded something heavy. It bounced from the ground as if jumping upwards and then slid a few paces in Katrusia's direction on the slippery and slanted surface of the ground.

Two paces from Katrusia on the ground lay the body of a hanged man. She gasped deeply and sharply; she wanted to run, but her feet stuck to the ground, and her eyes by themselves were welded to the body's frightening face. Its eyes protruded, full of the fear of death, a long tongue stuck out, mouth open wide in a frightening convulsion, with bared teeth, strong and healthy. The man had reddish hair on his head, with a similar brush on the chin, and greenish cheeks. The bare, thin neck wore a rope which, being cut short, dangled on his chest. He was poorly dressed in a dirty blue shirt and pants. On his chest was a large wooden board on which something was written in black letters on a yellow background.

From where did he fall? Katrusia raised her eyes and saw a ladder leaning against a telegraph pole; on the ladder stood a uniformed German, pocketing a knife. Above his head swung a piece of rope, the other end of which was fastened to the top of the pole.

The crowd, which at the moment of the body's fall gasped and split in two, now slowly streamed together, gathering around the body. Numb with shock, Katrusia was jostled by the crowd; she mechanically took a few steps to the side, not breaking her gaze from the frightening face of the hanged man. The people also silently examined him, captured by the same silent hypnotic horror. Only then did Katrusia catch with her eyes the meaning of those few words written in black letters on the board fastened to the dead man's chest: "I sold human flesh."

Katrusia with difficulty pushed her way out of the crowd and ran. Her feet carried her quickly, quickly, but in her head spun chaotic layers of fragmented, seared thoughts. They twirled like dry leaves following the wind, one replacing the other.

She had heard that in Kharkiv there had been cases of cannibalism, that someone was apprehended in the bazaar with sausages made from human flesh, and that someone had been hung for cannibalism, but she did not believe, did not want to believe those horrible rumors.

"The Germans hung in the bazaar a seller of human flesh," thought Katrusia as she ran home. "In this manner the German authorities 'help' the people not to die of hunger. But the population, suffering hunger and impoverished, creates for itself a new bestial 'morality,' which states: 'Everything is good which provides the opportunity not to die of hunger.' In the extreme stages of starvation, an extreme but quite logical conclusion of this new bestial 'morality' is cannibalism."

Katrusia ran; thoughts incomprehensible nervously spun in her head, and before her eyes floated the grotesque and horrible face of the hanged man, not going away.

Among other things, pregnant women should avoid gross and horrible impressions; Katrusia knew this well. She also knew that pregnant women need a warm dwelling, a healthy environment, healthy food, vitamins, and many other things.

A pleasant February day…. The frost has released some of its hold, snowflakes seldom fly, and the sun sends the impoverished and hungry Kharkiv residents its still-cold though full-of-spring smiles…. In these smiles from the February sun shine the premonition of spring, hope for life, for being saved….

Katrusia walked on the sunny side of Myronosytsky Lane, exposing her emaciated face to the first spring rays. At the eleventh doorway she stopped and awkwardly searched for a sign or a house number. The Shevchenko Gallery was in this building, but there were no notices about gold purchases here. Her neighbor had told her that this was where she could sell her gold ring. Katrusia shyly pushed against the heavy entrance doors and entered timidly. Empty. No one there. Beautiful marble stairs led upstairs; Katrusia, with mute questioning in her eyes, climbed the stairs, looking for notices or announcements on the walls, but the walls were bare.

Reaching the first floor, she approached the door on the right. Locked. She tried the door on the left. Open. She opened the door and joined a large crowd of people. Taking a closer look, she saw that these people belonged to the same category as she did. All were impoverished and poorly-dressed, with hunger's earmark on their emaciated, whitish-yellow faces. This meant that she was in the right place. People stood in a queue which filled the half-dark reception room with living bodies. The queue extended into the neighboring room, into which both halves of the door were open.

After getting used to the semi-darkness in the reception room, Katrusia saw that people were handing in their gold and precious items, and that accepting them was a squat man, who resembled a dark mushroom with a sated, tanned face. The man looked at the items and evaluated them behind a table that stood in the doorway of the neighboring room.

An old lady placed a gold chain on the table. The squat man weighed it and brusquely said, "A thousand rubles. Agreed?" She agreed, and the man allowed her inside, where he counted out the money and placed the chain in a showcase adapted from an older one. Because the room was bright and had large windows, the display case full of valuables could be seen from the reception room. Next, a young woman, withered thin like a board, placed a ring with diamonds on the table. The squat mushroom man carefully examined the diamonds with his jeweller's glass and bluntly said, "Two thousand. Agreed?" "No," said the woman. "It is worth more." "Next!" The man turned to a young girl who was fumbling with a small box, trying to get a ring out. The queue quickly moved forward.

Suddenly on the stairs heavy footsteps were heard, as well as German voices and German laughter; in the dark reception room appeared the shining figures of two German officers. The miserable common people who filled the room scurried out of the way, crushing one another, and the officers, gaily conversing, entered the room and went straight to the table.

The squat man immediately abandoned the girl with the ring and ran to satisfy the demands of his highly distinguished guests. Speaking in German, he showed his newly-gotten valuables to the officers. The officers were looking for two rings for themselves, rings being a big fashion craze amongst the German soldiers, and the squat man, without wasting time or fancy words, showed them his rings.

Where had they gone, his laconic manner and strict judge's tone? He, who could not see you, made decisions about your future as he evaluated each item that appeared before him. Now with his paying customers, he cooed like a male dove beside his hen, measuring a ring on the officer's finger, and his voice rang generously. He was friendly, for now he was not wasting his valuable time.

Half an hour passed, but the officers still had not selected rings for themselves. The line of hungry gold owners respectfully waited. Next to Katrusia stood a small man dried to the state of mummification; he was very talkative, and from him Katrusia learned what type of order ruled the buying and selling of valuables. In the building, the Shevchenko Art Gallery was housed; here there was a continuous exhibit of paintings, which the artists displayed for exhibit and sale; the Germans were the only buyers of such valuables as paintings. However, near the Gallery, some enterprising people placed on exhibit gold, diamonds, and other valuables bought from the population. Understandably, these goods enticed the Germans more than the paintings.

"Then why are there so few Germans here?" asked Katrusia.

"Because this is not the hour to serve Germans. There are definite hours for accepting gold from the population, but the sale of this gold to the Germans is undertaken at a different time. The breakdown of hours is on the doors of the room in which the gold is accepted. Take a look at this sign here on the door," said the talkative old man, pointing to a piece of paper that hung on the open door's outer side.

"And I was searching outside for some sort of an announcement about accepting gold," Katrusia said.

"Such a notice is completely absent and cannot exist; from the outside this is the Shevchenko Art Gallery. But what's inside, you can see for yourself," the old man explained to Katrusia didactically.

"Yes, I see what is inside, and among other things, I see two German officers who buy gold at the time allotted for accepting it from the people," said Katrusia, outraged. It was hard and cold for her, and there was nowhere to sit.

"Hee, hee, hee! What do you want, honorable do-gooder, to insinuate that this situation does not appeal to you?" laughed the old man heartily, in the old style. "Try to come here at the hour allotted to the Germans, and they will show you the door, but if the Germans come at the hours allotted for us, the buyers will leave us and serve them."

The old gentleman pushed aside a large painting wrapped in a bedspread, which he had brought to sell, and made Katrusia some space by the wall. "Here, lean against the wall. It will be easier for you to stand. You look very bad," the old man said with a sympathetic note.

"Thank you," Katrusia answered, and taking the space by the wall with the painting, asked: "You said yourself that the Germans are more interested in gold and diamonds than in artistic paintings. But you brought such a large painting, and if they don't accept it, then you will have to trudge it home by foot. Do you have at least a sleigh with you?"

"This painting won't have to be trudged home. The Germans seize such goods with their hands and pay richly."

"Who is the artist, then?" asked Katrusia.

"This painting is by an artist that nobody knows and, as such, that is unimportant. In this picture, naked ladies are painted, and the picture is called 'The Bathers.' Now do you understand the situation?"

"Yes I understand," Katrusia slowly said; she felt that she was really beginning to understand some things.

In the room a stir was created at that moment. People moved to make room for the departing German officers, who had finally bought rings for themselves. Again the queue reformed and the squat man, the receiver, again started working — categorically, quietly, unsinning in his evaluations, just like God. He must be given his due; he worked efficiently, and the line moved very quickly forward.

Finally the old gentleman placed his painting on the table and theatrically removed its cover. Before the eyes of all, there appeared three naked ladies bathing in a river. One was up to her waist in the water, while the others were bent in enticing poses on the banks, under the sun. On the canvas was depicted lush greenery, with a huge tree on the riverbank.

The old gentleman watched to see the reaction his painting would elicit from the squat receiver, who captured it with a quick glance and said in his brusque manner, "This painting will sell. Two thousand. Agreed?"

The old gentleman condescendingly laughed with his aged laughter and started to cover his painting with the bed sheet in preparation for departure. This had the intended effect.

"How much do you want?" asked the buyer, in a more businesslike voice.

"Five thousand and not a ruble less," firmly stated the old man, determinedly taking the painting from the table. The old man's determination forced the squat receiver to make a compromise.

"My proposition is this," he said. "You leave the painting in the gallery, and I will show it to the Germans. No one will give you five thousand rubles, but maybe I will be lucky enough to sell it for food. Come back in a week, and I will tell you how much and what type of food they are offering. If the painting is sold, I get ten percent commission. Agreed?"

"Agreed," and they shook hands.

"Next!" the receiver nodded to Katrusia. On the table the old ring made of red gold with three diamonds was obediently placed.

Glancing at the ring owner's face and calculating the extreme need in its appearance, he said: "Two thousand. Agreed?"

"No." Katrusia picked up the ring.

"Two and a half thousand? Agreed?"

"No, I am not agreed," said Katrusia. She put the ring in her pocket and turned for the door.

"Three thousand rubles!" yelled the receiver at her in pursuit.

Katrusia did not return. Rushing down the stairs angrily, she thought: "How quickly he jumped from two to three thousand! No! I will not let any speculator profit. I will not give any speculator that bread which belongs to me! I am now secure with food for a week, and I will not be too lazy to go to all the jewellery stores in Kharkiv, in order to find the place where they will give me the highest price."

In half an hour, Katrusia stood in line at a jewellery store on Shumsky Street, the same store Assistant Professor Vsevolod had directed her attention to.

The line of people, with their gold, formed at the side doors, down a half-dark corridor; people slowly moved through the doors to a room where the assessor accepted gold from them and paid for it. From the side room, the gold was carried to the store, where it was sold to the Germans, who entered through decorative doors on the main street. Gold, in a thin but unstoppable stream, flowed through the side door and in the same stream flowed out through the fancy doors. In the line at the side door stood Katrusia; she too was forced to add a golden drop with three clear-as-water tears, diamonds, to the unending stream of gold that flowed from the nearly-empty pockets of the hungry population into the bulging pockets of the German soldiers.

"Where is that German woman who will wear our family treasure?" bitterly thought Katrusia, nearing the appraiser's table. He was tall and old, and categorically knowledgeable in his relations with the hungry population, just like the squat mushroom man, the receiver at the Shevchenko Art Gallery. He spoke to the hungry gold suppliers with an underlined nuance of his superiority over them. "And why not? This is truly a persona grata," thought Katrusia. "He assists in the process of mining gold from the starving population's bosom and transports it into German pockets. Honorable work; here is something to be proud of!"

Katrusia placed her family treasure on the table and glared at the appraiser, who on his side also cast an evaluating glance at her. Katrusia understood that an impoverished look markedly lowers a ring's value and guardedly, angrily waited. The appraiser weighed the ring, looked through his jeweller's glass at the diamonds and said, "Two thousand."

"You will not give two and a half thousand?" angrily asked Katrusia. The appraiser glanced up at her sharply, then once again looked at the diamonds with his glass and brought out the money in order to count out two and a half thousand. Katrusia only laughed and said, "Look more carefully; maybe you will give three thousand rubles!"

The appraiser was insulted; he finally felt the irony in this miserable client's tone. But, at the same time, it would be a shame to let this interesting ring slip out of his hands. He restrained and calmed himself, and in a businesslike manner asked, "Tell me, how much do you want?"

"Five thousand," replied Katrusia.

"Well then, stay healthy and wear it yourself!" the appraiser said, clearly angered.

"Stay healthy!" Katrusia repeated. She took the ring and departed.

Having been to two other jewellery stores on Shumsky Street, Katrusia convinced herself that the buyers would not give more than three thousand. It was getting late; Katrusia felt hungry and tired, and decided to go home, where she could satisfy her hunger with the food bought yesterday, and to relax.

Slowly she walked along Shumsky, passing the snow-covered stretches of Profspilchansky Park, putting together a plan for herself; where would she go with her treasure tomorrow?

"Katrusia! Is that you?" A tall, strongly-built girl grabbed her, small and thin, in her arms and kissed her fervently on both cheeks.

"Where did you come from, Nastia? I so wanted to see you! I went to your place, but your neighbor told me that you had moved somewhere, but where, she did not know."

"I actually did move to my old aunt's, who was severely impoverished and almost died of hunger. Now we live together and somehow manage. Among other things, I now live much closer to you."

Katrusia carefully examined her friend. Nastia was a student in the same faculty and level as Katrusia. Her face had substantially thinned, but it had become prettier than previously, when Nastia had been overweight. Her figure had also become more compact; this also made her prettier. If it weren't for her 'potato nose,' Nastia would have been a very attractive girl. She was dressed modestly as always, with a tinge of strictness in her wardrobe's colors and styles. Her eyes shone with a brave, youthful lightning.

Had this strict, honorable and hardworking Nastia also become a German's lover? There was no sign of starvation on her. This question so interested Katrusia that she openly asked, "What have you been living on during the four months under the Germans?"

"I'll eagerly tell you, Katrusia," Nastia said honestly. "In the beginning of December, so as not to starve, I carried my things to the village to trade for food; with great difficulty I traded some, but with greater difficulty I carried the rest back on foot, sixty-three kilometers, to Kharkiv. You know that I am physically strong, but due to the hunger, I had lost my strength, and because of that, the road to Kharkiv with a load seemed so ominous.

"At a guard post near Kharkiv, the German guards took everything I had: some bacon, butter, eggs and also a wonderful live hen which I wanted to keep, because she laid eggs. I yelled and cried! I did not want to give it to them, and they beat me hard for that. And was it only me? They did the same with everyone who carried something valuable. So I returned home, with only a small amount of potatoes, losing all my better things and the food obtained for them. I returned home hungry, angry, exhausted by the hard journey and even beaten! Again the starvation began.

"Even though, Katrusia, I never was as beautiful as you, I had many shameful propositions from the Germans, the cynicism of which, according to my dignity, enraged me as a Ukrainian and as a woman. I can imagine how many similar propositions you must have had! At the same time, my aunt, who lived alone, was severely starving and lay swollen. I moved into her home, even though at that time, I did not know how I was going to save her. I simply thought that in such extreme poverty we must as relatives be together.

"One day, quite by accident, a begrimed German soldier asked me on a street if I knew who could wash his clothes for him, for a loaf of bread. He had with him his dirty underwear and a loaf of German bread. I said that I would wash it, and really, I washed it, even though the underwear was full of fleas, filthy and stinking; the stench from it would have racked your soul! From that time, Katrusia, my new career started. I am washerwoman for some German stableboys. Yes, just for the stableboys, because that dirty soldier boy turned out to be a stableboy, and now all his friends, also stableboys, bring me their underwear. They're satisfied with me, and I with them. You know, I'm convinced that the simple German soldiers have some heart in them, some humanity; sometimes they're even capable of feeling pity for us, the starving. But all sorts of 'Feldweble' and still more the officers, look upon us as cattle, and if more of that cattle croaks, the better.

"In order to finish about me, I'll tell you that by taking in underwear, I saved my aunt from starvation, and together we now manage around the house. She does all the housework, while I wash. I am physically very strong, and this gives me the ability to handle such hard work. I do not only wash; I carry wood on my back which I dig out of the ruins of bombed buildings. By myself I saw and I chop. If I lived by myself I would be afraid of letting soldiers into the house when they come to exchange their dirty clothing for the clean, but the appearance in the house of an old lady protects me from any possible aggression from my clients, the stableboys."

Nastia laughed, showing strong teeth. Her little potato nose wrinkled with laughter, but the dark eyes shone with fire, satisfied with their having conquered life's difficulties.

"You are a brave one!" admiringly said Katrusia. "I'm so happy that you didn't embark on that shameful road selling your body to the Germans! And do you know where Darochka lives? But first let us sit on the bench, because I feel weak, and cannot walk nor stand."

The two friends while talking stood by Profspilchansky Park; now they ventured inside and sat on a bench, from which they dusted off the snow like an owner would.

"You ask about Darochka? I saw her a week ago on the street, just as accidentally as you. Darochka has a coiffure with curls down her back and has two rings on each hand. She asked how I'm living. I told her that I wash the stableboys' underwear, and she twisted her painted mouth and said; 'Poor, Nastia, you are so poor, while I live so well. The Germans bring preserves, sausages, white bread, chocolate, sheer stockings and even these rings which you see on my hands. These are all German gifts!'

"Darochka was so proud of these German gifts that I became ill listening to her. And you know how open I am. I couldn't take it and I told her; 'Poor, Darka, you are poor! You yourself have not felt how low you have fallen, the shame with which you have covered your head! You proudly show off your German gifts, while I find it shameful to listen to you. I am red-faced for you, as a Ukrainian and as a woman, that you took such a miserable path. It would be interesting to know why these Germans are bringing such valuable gifts to you? Maybe because you are so smart? Maybe because you are called Darka and not Nastia?' That is how I talked to her. She burst into flames, evidently not completely lost, and left silently, but I still managed to yell after her: 'Come to your senses, Darka!'"

"You're a brave one to out-talk her!" Katrusia said with admiration. "It is not without reason that I liked you the most of all the girls in our course. I like you still more now. And how is Olya living?"

Nastia at this time brought something out of her bag, unwrapped it and slowly asked, "Olya? Which Olya? Ah, Olya Chmil. She has become a translator for the Germans."

Nastia held a large slice of German bread folded in two and buttered in the center; she broke it into two uneven halves and gave the bigger piece to Katrusia, with sincere sympathy saying: "Here, strengthen yourself, Katrusia. You look so frightful! If it weren't for your stringy eyebrows that everybody notices, I would not have recognized you."

Katrusia took the bread and began to break off only a small piece for herself. Nastia was sincerely insulted. "What do you think? Eat it all! This bread and butter are earned through the hard but honorable work of a washerwoman, and it is my pleasure to treat you with it."

For some minutes they both seriously and silently ate the bread and butter and Katrusia remembered another piece of bread and butter, with sausage even, with which Halya had treated her, and which was obtained through a woman's shameful lowering; such was Fritz's payment for Halya's body.

"Well now, no more words about our student-friends; now I would like to hear your story, though your appearance tells me you also did not follow the shameful path, though you probably had plenty of propositions."

Katrusia talked about herself, about Vasyl who had not returned, about her promise to him, about the pregnancy, about the hunger, about Assistant Professor Vsevolod, and about the ring. Tired of long solitude, she was glad that she could finally empty her soul. Nastia listened, and her dark eyes showed pity, sympathy, a sincere desire to help Katrusia.

The high-quality gold ring with three diamonds sat in Nastia's hands; she carefully examined it and said: "And some German woman has to wear this treasure on her hand! Take care, Katrusia; don't sell it too cheaply. And don't let the speculators profit from your poverty. When you've eaten those thousand rubles that the assistant professor gave you, then come see me. You will always get a loaf of bread for a week and some butter for Tarasyk from me. Throw away your false modesty; we are the same people and all have to help one another in trouble. Today you're in trouble, but tomorrow I may end up worse. We are young and before us spreads the long road into the unknown future. Even if you become indebted to me, the time will come for you to return that debt, if not to me, then to some other person who has ended up in trouble. Write down my address and come once a week for bread and butter. I am strong, and nothing will happen to me if I wash an extra set of underwear."

Nastia's proposition was stated so simply and so sincerely that Katrusia felt her soul warmed, and suddenly it was not so fearful to look into the future. Definitely, she would try to get out of her difficult predicament through her own power, but in an extreme case, Nastia's proposition guaranteed some extra leeway. She squeezed Nastia's large hand and quietly said just two words: "Thank you!"

Leaving the park, the friends walked in opposite directions, Nastia toward the center of town, and Katrusia to Shumsky Street, and then across Myronosytsky Lane to her home.

Walking by Shevchenko Art Gallery, Katrusia with interest looked over the shining German officers who stood gaily conversing on the steps. A car drove up, from which a German general alit in the company of two officers. All three disappeared behind the heavy decorative gallery doors. One could imagine what kind of tender dove the squat mushroom gentleman appraiser would be before the general, not limiting fancy words and time.

Maybe the painting 'The Bathers' by the unknown artist would be to the German general's liking. Who knows? It was the hour for serving Germans; it was the hour when the golden stream, decorated with clear, tear-like diamonds, flowed out of Shevchenko Art Gallery into German pockets, and from there to Germany, to the Reich.

A few days passed. During this time, Katrusia managed to visit all the jewellery and commission stores in Kharkiv. As a matter of fact, at this time in Kharkiv there were no other types of stores. They were all the same;

throughout ruled the same order, throughout appraisers were proudly and grandly categorical in their relations with the population. Each of these stores was a little well which provided gold for the Germans. The so-called 'black market' was located on the corner of Pavlivsky and Mykolajivsky Squares, where gold was bought not just by the speculators for the Germans, but even by the Germans themselves, directly from the population. Katrusia visited the black market, but did not sell her treasure; she merely established its value. More than three and a half thousand nobody offered. Having visited all the spots officially buying gold, she impressed on herself how Kharkiv's starving population supplied the Germans with gold.

Katrusia saw how gold streams with bright drops of clear diamonds on their shiny yellow bodies flowed out of each jewellery store and joined together, creating a golden stream which was directed from starving Kharkiv to the German Reich. Every starving Ukrainian city was the source of a similar stream. Ukraine was hungry, ruined, wasted, destroyed by war. Ukraine, it seemed to Katrusia, was a high, high mountain from which wild golden streams flowed, falling from a sheer height. They joined together in their travels and wildly, like a full-crested river, flowed into Germany. This river's water was shimmering yellow, and playing in it were bright-clear flashes of various sizes, blinding drops, our people's tears, tortured with hunger and tragedy.

Katrusia felt a need to inform Assistant Professor Vsevolod about her travels through all the Kharkiv jewellery stores, and she sought him out that day.

The assistant professor had just finished seeing his patients, and the two of them sat together comfortably behind his writing desk. He listened to her carefully and took from his side pocket a piece of paper which he placed before Katrusia's eyes.

"This is the address of a lady who buys the best and most expensive valuables for high-ranking German dignitaries and pays with wheat flour, sugar, even bacon. She is a great speculative fish who has a staff of several smaller speculators for relations with the public. She successfully competes with the stores, because she pays for the valuables somewhat generously, taking into consideration their artistic merit, rarity, age, and such. Because of this, the most interesting rarities come to her, and she serves the German military cream."

"You have this grand speculative fish's address and added to this, such detailed information about her? This does not conform with your academic interests nor with your dislike for the speculators."

"Hmm. How to explain to you, Katrusia? Such a lady has a certain relationship to the hunger problem, but that is not the issue. Simply avail yourself of her services. One of her agents is my patient, and that is how I obtained her address. Go to her with your treasure today, right now."

"Good," said Katrusia; she was used to heeding the advice of the assistant professor. She looked at the address. "This is not far from my building, near the vicinity of Pushkin Cemetery. I did not know that in such proximity to me was such a solid well for supplying the German cream with gold. I'll immediately go to this lady."

"I have two small observations to add to what I have already told you," said the assistant professor. "First, when the door is opened to you by the servant, tell her that you came from Ivan Pavlovych. Second, do not be afraid to leave your treasure with the lady overnight. It will not be lost. Only at night, when for us sinners it is forbidden to be on the street, do the German officers gather at her place to examine her valuables."

"Thank you for both warnings, especially for the second; if it weren't for your word, I would not leave my ring with her overnight."

"The thing is, Katrusia, that this lady has so profited from her operations that she buys diamonds even for herself. But no one knows how much the Germans pay her, because nobody other than herself sees these Germans. And she pays the client with German products, however much she feels is needed. This, you see, in their speculator's jargon is called 'to profit.' Therefore, profiting, she robs you as she wants, but to openly steal your item — this she would never do, because being a reputable speculator, she would be afraid of a scandal."

"This is all very interesting," said Katrusia, "and I am immediately going to see this lady. Thank you very much. Till next time!"

"Till next time, Katrusia. Good luck!"

"I am from Ivan Pavlovych," said Katrusia to the neatly-dressed servant, who measured Katrusia's figure from head to foot with her disrespectful glance. The girl disappeared, leaving Katrusia in the foyer and in a minute appeared again. She helped Katrusia with her coat, and opened the doors to the right, saying in a direct, controlled manner, "Please...."

In a neatly-decorated office, behind an elegant lady's writing-table, sat the lady, a small middle-aged woman with an average complexion. She was dressed in a black, elegant dress and her coiffure was luxurious. She obviously was knowledgeable and delicate in her use of cosmetics, and her small beautifully-framed hands were decorated with soft pink nails.

"Please wait a few moments," she said, motioning Katrusia with her hand to a chair, and continued her conversation with an old woman who sat across from her, and whose face Katrusia could not see.

"One hundred and sixty kilograms of wheat flour, regular grind, two kilograms of sugar, and two kilograms of bacon," said the lady, her voice pleasant and charming.

"No, I am not agreed," said the old woman. "This has thirty-seven diamonds! I am forced to take my valuable back." She stretched her hand and took something from the table.

Over the old woman's shoulder, Katrusia saw a six-pointed star; every point was made in the image of an arrow and six diamonds progressively became larger from the edge to the center; all six arrows met at a large central diamond of magnificent color.

"Truly, there are thirty-seven beautiful diamonds there," Katrusia calculated, and she stared, too weak to break her enraptured gaze from the wonderful play of the diamonds.

But the star was hidden in a box, the box was put into a bag and the old lady stood up. She was truly an old lady, probably at least seventy-five years old.

"It is awkward for me to bother you one more time," said the mistress with an enchanting smile, "but if it is not a problem, then drop in with your star the day after tomorrow in the morning. I will speak with whomever I can, and maybe we'll be able to obtain something more for you. Your final price?"

"Two kilos of sugar, two kilos of bacon, two hundred kilos of flour, and not a gram less!" said the client, and with an aged walk turned to the foyer. "Till next time."

"Till we meet the day after tomorrow in the morning," politely replied the mistress and called to the servant girl, "Marusia. Help the lady with her coat."

"Oh, this is a pleasant woman," Katrusia thought to herself. "It is too little to say that she is a 'simple pleasant lady.'" Using Mykola Gogol's words, she had to acknowledge that this lady was 'pleasant in all aspects.' It was not without reason that the German military cream employed her to trade for the most valuable rarities. They traded mostly wheat flour, made from the wheat that had grown in Ukrainian fields, and which was stored in warehouses to supply the German army.

The pleasant-in-all-aspects lady knowingly directed, with her little hands generously decorated with diamond bracelets, the golden stream to the pockets of the German officers, and the Ukrainian flour, marked for supplying the German army, to the temporary satisfaction of the insatiable needs of the hungry owners of the most valuable rarities.

"Why are your wonderful string eyebrows so strictly scowling, and about what are you so deep in thought?" the pleasant-in-all-aspects lady pleasantly asked Katrusia, and motioned her to the table.

Katrusia sat opposite the lady and silently placed the ring with the three diamonds on the table. The lady carefully examined it with her jeweller's glass, weighed it and put it on her stout little finger. On her stout, beautiful hands there were no rings, a small detail which fell into Katrusia's eyes. The lady for a long time examined her left hand with Katrusia's ring on the wrinkle-free stout finger. "An interesting ring," she said, "not at all ordinary. How much do you want for it?"

"How much will you give?"

"Sixteen kilograms of regular grind wheat flour," pleasantly offered the lady.

Katrusia reminded herself that the maximum the jewellers offered her was thirty-five hundred rubles, which equaled fourteen kilos of black bread. Therefore, the sixteen kilograms of wheat flour was already good. But, amazing herself with her bravery, Katrusia said: "I want twenty-four kilograms of flour."

"No one will give twenty-four," said the lady, with a pleasant determination. "But leave your ring with me for a night, and tomorrow I will give you a final price. Maybe this ring will appeal to some officer so much that he will give you more than sixteen. We shall see."

"Good, I shall return tomorrow morning." said Katrusia.

"Please do. Only not before ten o'clock." The audience finished, Katrusia left, while the ring with three diamonds remained on the fat wrinkle-free finger of the pleasant-in-all-aspects lady's left hand.

Katrusia had the impression that the 'great speculative fish' liked the ring and that she even regarded it as a possible item to decorate her own hand.

When the next morning at ten o'clock Katrusia again sat in the quiet office of the pleasant-in-all-aspects lady, she heard from her pleasant mouth a fairly pleasant price: twenty kilograms of flour. This pleased Katrusia, and she was ready to give her final word of agreement, when suddenly she was struck with an additional condition: "Of course, ten percent of that — that is, two kilograms — you are to pay me for commission, while eighteen kilograms is yours."

Though to this statement a sweet smile was added, Katrusia was enraged to the depths of her soul. "She is probably buying this ring for herself and she is still stealing from me two kilos of flour for her commission! In the speculators' jargon, this is called 'to profit,'" she reminded herself of Assistant Professor Vsevolod's words.

A deep, inborn, conscious contempt for the speculator was ready to break through with an insulting word, but Katrusia stopped herself, and with a forcibly calm tone said: "I want to discuss this further with an old relative. Please return my ring. If I agree, then I shall come to you, with your permission, tomorrow morning at ten o'clock."

The lady returned the ring and sweetly invited her to come tomorrow. "Nobody will give you more," she said with determination.

The day darkens.... Exhausted from the hunger and the rough times, Kharkivites sit, hammered into their poorly-lit, unheated holes, while in the city streets walk only people in green-blue uniforms....

Katrusia sat in her hole. She cooked potato-peel soup for herself, from another small pile of potato peels she had been lucky enough to buy from the same old grandmother at the bazaar. The peel soup boiled and bubbled, spreading everywhere the irritating aroma of boiled potatoes; on the table the oil lamp barely flickered while Katrusia sat on a little bench opposite the stove, adding minute wood splinters, and thought of many things: "Out of the home of this sweet lady, 'pleasant in all aspects,' flows a secret, rich, golden stream. In Kharkiv there must be other similar agents, who enrich themselves via the big golden stream that is directed from starving Kharkiv to the German Reich.

"It seems," she thought further, "that it must be finally time for me to add my contribution, a golden drop in the secret stream that flows from the house of the sweet lady. Maybe — who knows? — maybe my ring will stay in her house and become glued to her fat finger." Katrusia decided finally to take her ring in at ten o'clock. "More than eighteen kilos, no one will give."

A sharp knock at the door forced Katrusia to stand up from the stove. "Mrs Katrusia! Open the door! A German has come to you!" she heard her neighbor's familiar voice. In this voice rang amazement and even satisfaction, that a German finally came even to the untouchable Mrs Katrusia.

"For me, a German?" asked Katrusia, bewildered, as she opened the door. On the doorstep, truly stood a large rotund German.

"Good evening Mrs," he said in German and firmly crossed the doorstep of Katrusia's home.

Katrusia, confused, stepped back and with widely-opened eyes examined his simple, fat face and robust figure.

Curious about such an interesting event, the neighbor pushed her nose into the room and with an unfriendly-sweet voice asked, "Maybe I should lend you my lamp? It is not practical to host such a guest by an oil lamp."

"No, thank you," Katrusia angrily answered her and locked the door. "You probably are mistaken, sir," she said, turning to the German. "You came to the wrong address. Who do you need to see?"

The German pronounced her name in a fractured manner.

"Please sit," Katrusia with difficulty squeezed out of herself.

The German sat.

"What do you need?" Katrusia asked him.

The German went into his shirt, brought out a piece of paper and gave it to Katrusia. Bending over the oil lamp, Katrusia tensed and with emotion began to read.

"Katrusia!" she read. "This fat German is an old stableboy. He received an order from his fiancée to buy her a ring and not without diamonds. He has searched for a long time and cannot find it. Rip the most you can from this son of a devil! Don't worry; I can write what I want, because he won't be able to read my writing. For, whatever the case, I am telling you that he can pay with oats and wheat. He gets a certain amount for the horses, but as a stablehand, he can give it to you, and not to the horses. Ask no less than two pails of wheat and two pails of oats. I think that he may be able to bring you a portion of soup each day for a while, because his friend works as a cook and can pour him somewhat more each day. I wash for these 'Kamaraden' and their mutual relations are known to me. I am writing in detail for you because I fear that you, my little one, will irrevocably miss something and will sell your ring too cheaply.

"Your Nastia. P.S. His kitchen is not far from your building, so he can bring you some soup every day. It is almost on the way for him.

"Stay strong, Katrusia. Remember, the more you rip from him, the better it will be for your little Tarasyk!"

Katrusia, having read the note with interest, examined the fat, pockmarked face of the old stablehand; she was completely in control of herself. Oh, what a bridegroom this was who came for a family valuable!

The soldier asked to see the ring. Katrusia placed the box by the oil lamp and followed the movements and face of her guest.

With difficulty he opened the small box and placed the ring on the palm of his right hand.

He stared at it for a long, long time, while the oil lamp, Katrusia's partner, flickered; in the dancing light of the flickering, the diamonds played enticingly, secretly changing, glimmering. They soothed the primitive heart of the stablehand, and he, not hiding his enchantment, hoarsely said: "Den Ring kaufe ich!" and pointed a dirty finger with a black nail to his own stout, broad breast.

This finger was to convince Katrusia that only he, and no one else, would have the ring. He said that tomorrow they both would go to a jeweller, who would confirm to the old stablehand that the diamonds were real, and then he would buy. Oh, he had the means to pay; Katrusia must not worry about that; he was a stablehand in the German army.

"Tomorrow, to the jeweller's," Katrusia said, laughing, and proposed that they go there together with Nastia.

The old stablehand said, "Nashta ich bin ein gutes Madchen."

The two agreed on ten o'clock the next morning when he, together with Nastia, would wait for Katrusia by the jewellery store on Mykolajivsky Square. Katrusia hid her treasure in its box and the German said, "Gute Nacht," turned to the door and departed.

Katrusia accompanied him along the corridor to close the entry doors after him. The neighbor, still interested in the uncommon event, poked her nose from her door and watched. "Your guest is going so soon?"

"As you see!" chopped Katrusia.

The next day, having been convinced by the jeweller that the diamonds were real, the old stablehand eagerly announced his decision to Katrusia and Nastia. Only he will have this ring, and no one else!

The three of them went to Katrusia's and began to discuss the most difficult question of the ring's price. The old stablehand had heard the jeweller appraise the ring at thirty-five hundred rubles; this made an impression on him of a great price, but in the area of finance, he obviously was not well-versed.

Nastia played a large role in this transaction. She capably portrayed herself as an objective judge, but all the time 'drove the water' toward Katrusia's 'mill.' Two hours of negotiations brought an agreement.

The old stablehand would give Katrusia two pails of wheat and two pails of oats; for a whole month he was to bring, each day, a serving of soldier's soup and a piece of bread not smaller than one hundred grams. The ring would be held by Nastia and she would give it to the old stablehand in one month, after Katrusia had attested that everything according to the deal had been received. The old stablehand promised to bring the first pail of wheat to her that very evening.

Katrusia could barely contain her wild happiness within herself; when the robust figure of the old stablehand had disappeared through the doors, she threw herself at Nastia, who again held the starved Katrusia in her strong hands, and threw her like a feather onto the bed. Katrusia shook with happiness, trembled, shivered and kissed Nastia's cheeks and face. Even Nastia's potato nose received a few extremely hot kisses.

"Quieter, quieter, I beg you! Crazy woman! You may hurt your Tarasyk!" Nastia scolded her, also laughing happily.

Days passed after days. Katrusia shared her happiness with the assistant professor and received from him a list of helpful advice on how to rehabilitate herself with the food from the German. The stablehand kept his word and immediately brought a large pail of magnificent wheat and in a few days a pail of oats. Every day at one o'clock he knocked at the window and Katrusia ran out to the porch; he poured a thick soldier's soup into her bowl and gave her a piece of bread.

Katrusia began to revive; the swelling on her feet and beneath her eyes disappeared. Her face gained a more lifelike appearance with each passing day.

It was the beginning of March and five months of pregnancy had passed. When she felt her Tarasyk's movements in her, she became solemnly serious, concentrating on this barely-felt movement, and she said to herself, "Now he moved his feet, or was it his hands?" Sorrowfully and hopelessly her heart longed for Vasyl. When the pain of hunger lessened, the soul's hurts made themselves felt even more.

One evening, while she ate gruel cooked from the oats, the old stablehand knocked at her door; he brought the second pail of wheat, according to the agreement.

Katrusia emptied the pail and invited her guest to sit. By this time, she had learned his name, and the two were on fairly friendly terms. "You know, Herr Hans," Katrusia said, "I am interested in how your fiancée looks. Do you maybe have her photograph?"

Herr Hans did not have to be asked twice. He eagerly brought a worn photograph out of his pocket. By the light of the oil lamp, Katrusia with interest looked at a robust, awkward girl with a fat, animal face and a square body, without any hint of a waist. "Truly a mutt!" she thought to herself, but aloud declared the girl to be very pretty.

"Here is the person who will wear our family treasure on her finger!" she wanted to scream with anguish. "Why does this have to be so?"

"And please tell me Herr Hans," she said, returning the photograph to the old stablehand, "you will soon receive the ring. How will you send it to your fiancée? It is such a small item and can be lost in the mail." She asked this with artificial naïveté. In fact, she wanted to know how the golden stream flowed out of hungry Kharkiv.

"Oh, there is no problem. It is done very simply. I am mailing a valuable item, not for the first time, and I know how it is done," proudly answered the old stablehand.

"In Kharkiv, as in every city, is an office which undertakes the sending of gold to the Reich. I appear with the item I want sent and I fill out a special form with the address of my fiancée. In my presence my valuable is packed into a small box, which has the same number as the accompanying form. When many such boxes are gathered, they are sorted according to the principal cities of Germany; those that are going to Leipzig, for example, are tightly packed into a large box which is directed to Leipzig. These bigger boxes of gold, each of which is directed to a specific city, are transported to Germany under a special guard; there they are sent to the cities and in the cities are delivered according to their addresses."

"So you are guaranteed that your fiancée will receive this ring?" asked Katrusia.

"Completely guaranteed. I have already written her about it and she awaits it. Now my next purchase will be two wedding rings. If any of your acquaintances has massive rings, then I may buy them."

"Good. I shall ask," answered Katrusia, thinking: "Why not? Why not, indeed! My family treasure is going to you completely gratis; you stole from the horses four pails of feed, and your Kamerade the cook poured you an extra ration of soldier's soup every day for a month.

"But who knows? The possibility is not ruled out that every day from now on you will bring me your leftovers and those of your friends!"

Editor's Note

Here the story ends. Did Katrusia find wedding rings for the stableboy? Did she thus join the army of speculators who profited from the greed of the German soldiers? Did she thus become part of the mechanism which directed the golden stream out of hungry Kharkiv?

Unfortunately, we will never know, as the writer of the original story is no longer with us, and this translation is the whole of her original manuscript. Our questions will remain unanswered, except for our own ideas of what the answers are.

—Danny Evanishen